DEATH AND THE COLLEGE STUDENT

A Collection of Brief Essays
on Death and Suicide
by Harvard Youth

Edited by
EDWIN S. SHNEIDMAN, Ph.D.
Professor of Medical Psychology
University of California at Los Angeles

Foreword by
Dana L. Farnsworth, M. D.
Henry K. Oliver Professor of Hygiene Emeritus, Harvard University;
Consultant on Psychiatry, Harvard School of Public Health

Behavioral Publications • New York

Library of Congress Catalog Card Number 72-2437
Standard Book Number
Paper: 87705-038-4
Cloth: 87705-083-X

Behavioral Publications, Inc.
72 Fifth Avenue
New York, New York 10011

Printed in the United States of America

Third Printing

Library of Congress Cataloging in Publication Data

Shneidman, Edwin S comp.
Death and the college student

CONTENTS: Death is alive and well in the ghetto, by B. F. Rose.—Hope and suicide in the concentration camp, by C. W. Beaver.—"Growing old": death by installment plan, by W. F. Scoggins. [etc.]
1. Suicide—Addresses, essays, lectures. 2. Death—Addresses, essays, lectures. I. Title.
HV6545.S354 364.1'522 72-2437

TO
JEANNE

Contents

FOREWORD

This series of students' essays on death and suicide tells as much about students as it does about the subjects on which they are writing--and that is one of the strong features of this book. Over and over again, the baleful effects of isolation, rejection, and lack of affection are revealed. When to these are added disillusionment and despair over present national and world conditions, it is not surprising that there is so much alienation and pessimism. As one of the student authors says, "If at death one sees no future hope it is because he has not created that hope in his life." This is consistent with the often-observed attitudes of dying persons--those who have lived satisfying and rewarding lives of service and accomplishment have far less fear of dying than those who have never managed to acquire faith and confidence that life has meaning and purpose.

These essays are of particular interest to me because the authors, and more than 15,000 other students, comprised the group whose health it was my responsibility (as Director of the Harvard University Health Services) to protect at that time. Prevention of student suicides is one of the highest priority goals of any college health service. The suicide rate at Harvard has varied considerably since reliable records have been available, ranging from one for every 5,090 student years (from 1946 to 1957), to one for every 10,250 students years (1958 to 1965), a reduction of 50%. Since that time, the rate has remained between those two extremes.

Contrary to what might have been expected, the rise of student despair, alienation, experimentation with drugs for recreation, loss of confidence, and disillusionment with societal modes of regulation has not caused a wave of suicides. Private hopelessness or despair, rather than distress concerning public developments that is shared with one's peer group, is the paramount motive for suicide.

Newspaper reporters like to spread the idea that major tension-producing events of the day are likely to increase the number of suicides among college students. The fact that suicide rates do not reflect the Vietnam war, student protest, increases in drug use or misuse, or any of the other major sources of student concern does not deter them from writing stories about the alarming increase in number of suicides among college students. In fact, major and recognizable sources of stress can be handled well by most youngsters. What they cannot tolerate is hopelessness, neglect, having no one who cares, or losing someone who does, especially when that person's love was apparently unique and irreplaceable.

If I were to simplify a very complex problem in a constructive way, based on my experience over nearly four decades of working with young people, I would say that the most important force or influence preventing a distraught young person (or anyone else) from trying to end his own life is a warm, trusting, dependable relationship with someone who cares deeply for his welfare and who can get across to him that this concern is genuine. For many college students, the college psychiatrist corresponds to that person. But for many others, such a relationship is not possible for various reasons, and the trusting and trusted person must be a teacher, a boy or girl friend, or someone who has frequent contact with the despairing individual. Hence, in my view, every community should have a number of persons in it who are aware of the depth, variety, power, and subtlety of self-destructive wishes and preoccupations and who are willing to save a life by responding when such a crisis becomes apparent. Pastors, physicians, psychologists, counselors, or informed and sensitive friends may do as much as psychiatrists in many instances. In any case, such individuals can do much to refer troubled persons to whatever more highly trained help is available.

Children can deal with the fact of death quite effectively if they are told explicitly, kindly, and sensitively what it means, and if an older person helps them deal with their grief. It is quite possible that children are not truthfully informed because of the lack of confidence, on the part of parents and others, that children can tolerate seeing and feeling their own grief reactions. Mourning is as necessary for the child as for adults, though the nature and time sequence of the mourning reaction in children may be more variable.

Erikson, in his description of the eighth stage of life, integrity, said that "healthy children will not fear life if their elders have integrity enough not to fear death." Apparently Mozart must have developed some of this kind of integrity. At the age of 31, he wrote, "Since death (properly understood) is the true ultimate purpose of our life, I have for several years past made myself acquainted with this truest and best friend of mankind so that he has for me not only nothing terrifying anymore but much that is tranquillizing and consoling."

The discussions of death and destruction, while infinitely varied, frequently lead into its pathological variations. The labored comparisons of death with pornography leave me unimpressed, but they may well lead to a more mature and acceptable attitude later on.

The response to an experimental classified ad, placed by a young man in a newspaper widely read by young people and asking for reasons why he should not commit suicide, suggests that those who are willing to help in such situations are very numerous (Chapter 5).

One cannot read this book without learning much about death, suicide, and motives for self-destruction. Even more interesting, however, is the impressive variety of approaches to the subject by very astute observers, most of them not yet overburdened by personal tragedies. Any student of the way human beings deal with tragedy and the prospect of their own nonexistence will find this book both stimulating and illuminating.

Dana L. Farnsworth, M.D.

February, 1972
Boston, Massachusetts

PREFACE

This volume of readings is a collection of papers on death and related topics written by college youth.

Traditionally, youth is a disturbed time of life. But nowadays this fact is especially evident, moreso, say, than a generation or two ago. In defense of this assertion one can easily point to a number of externals: the development of the faddish use of drugs, the tensions within minority and majority groups, our lethal involvement abroad, and the existence of the super bomb (and its revolutionary effect on international stresses). All these are admittedly extremely potent forces and therefore need to be included in any total equation which purports to explicate the current "death scene."

But there are other perspectives from which the question can be approached. In a previous publication (1967), a notion of types of crises was outlined. Briefly, that presentation proposed that -- given the proposition (from Shakespeare, C.G. Jung, Ernest Schatchel, Charlotte Buhler, Gerald Heard, and Erik Erikson) that there are major "times" or epochs in each human life cycle (like childhood, youth, young adulthood, middle age, old age) -- one could distinguish among three different kinds of life crises: (a) those crises which occur _within_ a period of a life (e.g., during childhood), called _intratemporal_ crises; (b) those crises which occur _between_ any two consecutive periods of a life (e.g., in the turn or interstice between young adulthood and middle age), called _intertemporal_ crises; and (c) those crises which occur _independent_ of one's time in life; crises which are seemingly content-free, but which, on further examination, are secondary or resonating to deeper issues and conflicts. These are metacrises, really. We call them _extratemporal_ crises.

Whereas intratemporal and intertemporal crises relate to individuals who are, for their chronological age, more-or-less in an appropriate phase of their lives, extratemporal crises relate to incidents which occur <u>out of phase</u> with life. This group includes individuals who have "too early" savored experiences "beyond their age" and, in this sense, are too old for their years (and are inappropriately precocious in life development); conversely, that group also includes individuals who are not "grown up emotionally," who are sheltered not only from experience but from contemplation (and are retarded in life's ways). These individuals are, in terms of their chronological age, out of tune with the modal psychological issues and conflicts that ought to be occupying their psyches. They are way ahead of themselves, or way behind. Experiences that come "too early" -- such as being orphaned at three, being seduced (and having to understand the impact of genital sexuality) at seven, or having to face annihilation (by being made aware of city-killing bombs) at nine -- put one dangerously out of phase with one's own years. These individuals suffer from "information overload" or what we might call"stimulus inundation." In any event, it is a heavy psychological burden.

Many suicidal acts, for example, reflect metacrises. That is to say, on the one hand, we hear reported almost every "reason" for suicide (ill health, being jilted, loss of fortune, pregnancy, loss of job, school grades, etc. -- some more persuasive than others) and, on the other hand, we hear of suicides for which "we simply cannot imagine why he did it." It may well be that in some cases the substantive reasons are simply not sufficient to explain the events. What seems to happen in these cases is that the individual becomes disturbed (over ill health, loss of work,etc.) and then develops a panic reaction (a metacrisis to his perception that he is in fact disturbed). He becomes agitated over the fact that he is anxious -- or anxious over the fact that he is agitated. At the time of the greatest perturbation, the specific content which sparked the original disturbance may not be recoverable to the mind. These metacrises may occur during any phase of life and are thus independent of the phase itself. Suicide may represent a panic reaction to the individual's feeling that things are getting out of control, a meta-critical act, representing a reverberating crisis, with its own autonomy. Erikson provides us with a quotation which clarifies this notion of the metacrisis: "This is the truth behind Franklin D. Roosevelt's simple yet magic statement that we have nothing to fear but fear itself, a statement which for the sake of our argument must be paraphrased to read: We have nothing to fear but anxiety. For it is not the fear of a danger (which we might be well able to meet with judicious action), but the fear of the associated states of aimless anxiety which drives us into irrational action, irrational flight -- or, indeed, irrational denial of danger."

Our principle assertion -- the key hypothesis which animates this volume -- is that many members of contemporary youth are caught in these extratemporal crisis situations. That is why so many young people appear, paradoxically, both advanced and retarded for their years; that is why easy answers are not forthcoming; that is why many youth seem, and are, out of phase with the staid world and, more importantly, out of phase with themselves.

The appropriate beneficent response -- one does well to avoid such terms as "treatment" or "remediation" -- to extratemporal crises requires special rules and unique understandings. In a grossly oversimplified way, ordinary stage-fright is a paradigm of a metacrisis. It is generally characterized by a state of rather free-floating anxiety in which the individual not only cannot do what he wishes or ought to do (i.e., to remember what it is he is supposed to say), but, more critically, he cannot attain that state of unvigilance, pacificity and equanimity that is a <u>sine qua non</u> to his beginning to remember what he has forgotten or blocked. Obviously, the first step to recovery --unless one elects to drop out-- is to reduce the level of affect (of anxiety, anger, fear, disillusionment, etc.) before the substantive issues (the content of the blocked material) can be dealt with in a more ordinary and "rational" way.

Thus so, the level of <u>angst</u> (or turmoil, despair, disillusionment, and fear) must be rolled back -- by disengaging from pointless wars, by reducing the felt anxiety over nuclear destruction, by achieving "purpose" and direction, and by having leaders who create rapport and inspire confidence (instead of the opposite). All these are preliminary to the alleviation of the metacrisis of this generation of youth.

With the sole exception of one chapter (chapter 4), all the papers for this collection were written by college undergraduates enrolled in a course on the Psychology of Death which I taught as Visiting Professor at Harvard in 1969.

From almost any point of view, the Spring 1969 semester at Harvard was one of considerable ferment. It was the semester of the University Hall take-over, the police bust, and the student strike -- all unique occurrences even in Harvard's 330-year history. A great deal happened there in those explosive months relative to the topic of death, including events which touched on the life and death of an institution.

For me, it was a period of extending my twenty-year long professional obsession with the topic of death -- dating from 1949, when I had adventitiously come upon hundreds of genuine suicide notes in the underground vaults of the Los Angeles County Coroner's Office . It was also, idiosyncratically, an especially death-oriented semester: Mornings I saw dying patients at the Massachusetts General Hospital, under the direction of Dr. Avery Weisman, and on certain afternoons and evenings I gave a course and conducted a seminar on Death and Suicide at the university.

The class was scheduled for a room with 20 chairs; over 200 students appeared for the first session. Thus the first task in the course was to reflect on the "popularity" of death. If one grants that, in our time, there is a new permissiveness -- even an urgency-- to deal with the topic of death, how then does one account for this? What the Harvard students teach us (and what I hope is reflected in this collected volume of their works) is that there are some discernible social and psychological forces which give impetus to this new orientation toward death.

As to the participants in this volume, some details are available about members of the class. A total of 155 students completed the course for credit. At the outset they sound atypical: Harvard and Radcliffe students - an admittedly special group -- who, for a variety of reasons elected to take a course on death.

"Demographically" the group can be characterized as follows: The age range was from 17 to 22; the median age for male was 20, for females 19. All but four members of the class, two men and two women (not married to each other) were single. All four years of college were represented; 40 per cent were freshman; the other three classes were about equally represented: 20, 15, and 25 per cent sophomores, juniors and seniors, respectively.

With only a few exceptions the students were Caucasian; a few were Oriental and a half-dozen were Negro. Sixty per cent of the group were Protestants (of twelve different denominations) and around twenty per cent each were Catholic and Jewish. According to their own statements (from a class questionnaire), -- the tenacity of their religious adherence ranged from atheist to pious. A few vignettes may give something of the spectrum: "A Presbyterian by heritage, a heretic by fact and a believer in death through fear." "My parents were Jewish. I have no religious affiliation. I am a typical New York City Jew. I like chopped liver but not gefulte fish." Typically, many of the responses of nineteen and twenty year olds reflected religious questioning, searching, lighting for a while, and sometimes finally settling.

A wide range of interests -- college majors and areas of concentration --was represented in the group: 30 per cent each from Social Relations and the Arts-Humanities; 20 per cent from Science and Mathematics; 15 per cent English; and 5 per cent other. Almost the entire spectrum of the Harvard-Radcliffe colleges was represented in the course.

In general, the family backgrounds are upper-middle class or upper-class. The students reported annual family incomes which averaged over $30,000. The range was from less than $5,000 to over $250,000 per year; very few reported incomes below $15,000. Comparisons with available information from previous Harvard classes (from the Harvard Alumni Review, December 23, 1968) indicated that the Death Class group was, at least in terms of socio-economic variables, rather typical of the Harvard population as a whole for the past several years.

With a small number of (conspicuous and inconspicuous) exceptions, the group was, by self-report, happy and well-adjusted. An interesting detail: The item " Current marital status of your parents," revealed that 14 per cent came from homes where there had been the disruption of divorce, death of the father, separation or the parents had never married.

More fascinating was that a large number of the respondents -- 25-- who checked that their parents were married, gratuitously added words like "happily," "successfully," "great" or "groovy." Unusual for these times! All this demonstrates that in life advantage, success and stability breed more of themselves.

Two sentences from the autobiography item might epitomize the group. From a 21 year old Harvard student: "Born in New York City, son of Har-Rad parents; grew up in a series of upper-middle class suburbs; private schools; Cape Cod Summers; planning a career in medicine; politically radical-liberal; fairly religious; civil libertarian on drugs and sex; what else can I say without going on for volumes?" And from a 21 year old Radcliffe student: "A major trait that characterizes my personality is the constant war I wage within myself between the worlds of adulthood and childhood; on the one hand I am strictly certain as to the moral code I accept and on what I would be but on the other I am fascinated by things that aren't always best for me; perhaps this is the female delight in self-suffering so greatly enhanced by the novels I used to read; I am a woman of today in love with the forgotten glitters of yesterday and the hidden secrets of tomorrow."

I am especially grateful to each student-author for giving me permission to reproduce his or her paper. In two instances -- although permission to print the paper and to use the author's name was freely and graciously given -- I deemed it better (even after changing possibly identifying details) to have the papers published anonymously. What was lost to these two young gifted people in pride of authorship is, I believe, balanced in the freedom they will have from being misunderstood by others at some future time. Them I thank doubly.

No assertions can be made for the "typicality" of this Harvard-Radcliffe group for U. S. youth in general. In many ways, these particular young people are (and proudly consider themselves) atypical. Many of them work hard at it. But there is a substantial area for the converse belief. In many ways, these advantaged youth live, share, exhibit (and sometimes express somewhat more articulately than most) the root questions and core problems of all contemporary youth. All the issues are there: drugs, sex, war, representation, action, identity, antipathy for Establishment, empathy for causes, the problems of adolescence-adulthood: finding and holding love, preparing for work, aspiring to accomplish one's own dreams. These are youth's problems everywhere.

While no one can pretend that, in many ways, this college group is not a special one, we should still keep in mind that a young and highly educated group of people -- perhaps a critical minority; a "cutting edge" of society -- may reveal where the rest of society is heading. We must beware of making the error of denying the broad areas of possible generalizability from these admittedly special data to today's youth in general, especially where they touch on the more ubiquitous aspects of life -- like death.

E.S.S.

Los Angeles, California
November, 1971

PART I

CONTEMPORARY CONTEMPLATIONS OF DEATH

Chapter 1

Death is Alive and Well in the Ghetto

Barbara F. Rose

When I was four my maternal grandfather died; I have no memory of the event. When I was around eight years old my paternal grandfather died; I remember some family commotion, nothing more. I must have been about fourteen when a very close friend of the family died; I instinctively knew it was going to happen. I was told, in velvet tones, that she had passed away, but I did not attend the funeral. I attended my first funeral when I was about seventeen. Pretty fuzzy memories.

On the first page of his book, Claude Brown, (1965, p.9) recollects a childhood experience:

"I ran. There was a bullet in me trying to take my life, all thirteen years of it.

I climbed up on the bar yelling, 'Walsh, I'm shot. I'm shot.' I could feel the blood running down my leg. Walsh, the fellow who operated the fish-and-chips joint, pushed me off the bar and onto the floor. I couldn't move now, but I was still completely conscious.

Walsh was saying, 'Git outta here, kid. I ain't got no time to play.'

. . . I began to think about dying. The worst part of dying was thinking about the things and the people that I'd never see again . . ."

These two, conceivably typical, examples illustrate the distinction which can be drawn between the "American" way of death and the ghetto way of life and death. One is struck by the frequency of the theme of death and dying which pervades "black literature," and the void of such discourse in middle class America. There is an essential significance in this difference, both for the psychologist and the sociologist. And it is to this difference that I wish to call attention.

At best, death suffers the same euphemistic treatment as excretion does in middle class American discourse. Both subjects are largely considered taboo for polite conversation and seem rarely to be the topic of serious discussion. Gorer (1965, p. 196) comments on this in his Appendix on the "Pornography of Death":

> The natural processes of corruption and decay have become disgusting, as disgusting as the natural processes of birth and copulation were a century ago; preoccupation about such processes is (or was) morbid and unhealthy, to be discouraged in all and punished in the young. Our great-grandparents were told that babies were found under gooseberry bushes or cabbages; our children are likely to be told that those who have passed on (fie! on the gross Anglo-Saxon monosyllable) are changed into flowers, or lie at rest in lovely gardens. The ugly facts are relentlessly hidden; the art of embalmers is an art of complete denial.

In the nineteenth century it was not uncommon for people to die at an early age from natural causes. Medical facilities being what they were, illness and death were more likely to have been a "household" experience rather than a hospital experience. "Children were encouraged to think about death, their own deaths and the edifying or cautionary death-beds of others." (Gorer, p. 195). Sex was the pornographic subject of the century. The tables are now turned and open discussion of sex is considered healthy. On the other hand, for the middle class American, death from natural causes has become the finitude of an ever-expanding future; while a violent death has become possible for all, but probably only "for the other guy." The fantasy of violence and death has replaced that of sex. Our concept of death is now a mutation of a formerly normal life process and philosophical enigma.

The ghetto knows no such luxury. The possibility of not only early death - natural or violent - but death at any time engraves the reality of death in ghetto life. Youth is not spared this knowledge. If anything, the adventures of youth uncover it. While recovering from the gunshot wound, Brown (p.12) has a nightmare which flashes vivid images of the role of death in his young life. He dreams of the time "Rock" and "Big Stoop" threw a boy off the roof of a building. "None of us had stayed around to see him hit the ground, but I just knew that he had died in a pool of blood, too." He dreams of the time his mother had to call the police to stop his father from beating Pimp, his younger brother. And he dreams (p.12) of the tenement in which he lives:

> This was the building where Mr. Lawson had killed a man for peeing in the hall. I remembered being afraid to go downstairs the morning after Mr. Lawson had busted that man's head open with a baseball bat. I could still see blood all over the hall. This was the building where somebody was always shooting out the windows in the hall. They were usually shooting at Johnny D., and they usually missed. This was the building that I loved more than anyplace else in the world. The thought that I would never see this building again scared the hell out of me.

The chance nature of many violent deaths forces the realization that everyone's lot is largely the same. There is equality of vulnerability in the ghetto. Anyone could die to support a junkie's habit. Everyone knows the risks, but different people try to beat the odds in different ways. Many live with the knowledge and offer little active resistance. Malcolm X's sister Ella is a good example. Others try to out-smart, out-talk, out-steal, out-run or out-fight the adversary . . .whomever, whatever and wherever it may be. But the fact remains that these are all ways of coping with death, not denying it.

Even though death is not a popular topic of conversation among middle class people, we cannot assume that this public denial of death extends completely into private lives. People do, indeed, think about death. Frederick Hoffman, in his essay "Mortality and Modern Literature," notes that there has been a general change from thinking of death as a beginning (religious grace, afterlife, etc.) to thinking of it as an end, as a consequence of twentieth century knowledge. Ongoing scientific advances are making the possibility of total destruction quite real, while at the same time making the plausibility of afterlife increasingly difficult to accept. Consequently, an awareness of death spawns thoughts of living one's only life to the fullest rather than living in preparation for the life after death.

Hoffman -- in Feifel's book (1959, p. 134) expresses this notion as follows:

> The more realistic ambitions of science were to eliminate disease, to facilitate movement, and to increase comfort. The first of these was a move toward the postponement of death; the second was supposed to reduce the incidence of human misunderstanding; the third was a step on the way to creating a surrogate heaven on earth.

Maslow's theory of self-actualization and the hierarchy of needs helps to explain why ghetto life precludes an awareness of death from being a sparkplug to seeking a fulfilling life. According to Maslow each individual has a hierarchy of needs through which he progresses step-wise, fulfilling the basic ones of physical health, safety, love and self-esteem before being able to confront the search for truth, beauty, honesty, etc. Affluence and material conveniences have enabled the average American to accommodate his physical needs; and the social mores based on this economy, by setting group norms for love and self-esteem, are abetting that pursuit. A ghetto resident, on the other hand, spends each day confronting the problems of food, shelter and health. The "surrogate heaven" our scientists are so busily creating is painfully visible and unattainable. Relative deprivation, then, is one reason that an awareness of death, rather than giving impetus and incentive, adds only impotence and futility to living.

We have discussed the fact that middle class Americans view death as the termination of their unique life, making urgent the establishment and pursuit of personal goals. This places death at the end of one person's life-time continuum. But life does go on; and people also tend to place their death on a longer time continuum, preceded by their life and followed by society's continued existence. Here, too, the influence of this perception differs according to the environment one lives in.

Although it may appear in contradiction with what I have stated previously, I propose that a middle class death is a futuristic one. It is true that knowledge and sophistication are undermining faith in an after-life (Hoffmann calls it "grace"); and the possibility of destroying ourselves, and with us the future of our world, increases with every press release from Washington and the Kremlin. Nonetheless, I feel that most middle class

Americans still have faith in a social future, even if it is only the faith that we will find a way to prevent the fate with which we threaten ourselves. Thus, we work not only to fulfill personal goals within our life, but also toward the betterment of future generations. Hoffmann (1959, p. 140) describes this as "social immortality":

> The secularization of man's self-judgment has had an important effect upon his view of grace. Grace is sometimes seen as health, physical or social. That is, it is what we deserve if we are "scientifically" or "verifiably" good. In this sense, personal immortality is dissolved into a social immortality. A state is progressively strengthened; evil is gradually purified out of it; and I as citizen, in working toward that future condition of bliss (not for myself but for my children's children), share posthumously in it.

This attitude about life/death fosters a cohesiveness, a link, a kind of universality . . . even a generational bridge, if you will, among the middle class. Individual enterprises and objectives terminate while the greater goal lives on.

The acceptability of this idea within the ghetto hinges on the word <u>change</u>. The requisite faith is put not just in the future, but in the hope for improvement. Four hundred years bear the frustration which has blockaded this faith. Each generation is really then no more than each man for himself. The pages of black literature are full of examples like these two from Brown (1965, p.10 & 190) and from Malcolm X (1964, p.126):

> Turk was standing there in the doorway hoping that I would die before I could tell the cops that he was with me.
>
> Cats were taking butcher knives and going at their fathers because they had to have money to get drugs.
>
> I'd also known of at least another dozen showdowns in which one took the Dead On Arrival ride to the morgue, and the other went to prison for manslaughter or the electric chair for murder.

To work in hope of a better future would mean turning

back the tide of a society which has been getting progressively worse. How can one think of trying to turn the tide when one's head is barely above water?

Twenty years ago the issue of social immortality was probably this clear-cut and the simplistic analysis I have proposed might have sufficed. However, times <u>have</u> changed (for the better?) and we now have a generation gap in addition to an economic one. The "coming of age" to social science as well as the whole of society requires that it be considered a significant social parameter in addition to its present role as a determinant of individual opinions. The two original groups under consideration were compared vertically according to economics (rich/poor) and resulting social and cultural environment (non-ghetto/ghetto). We find now that these two groups must be sub-divided according to age differences. Illustrated graphically, instead of having two groups separated by a horizontal line, we have four quadrants, each of which must be considered individually, even if only cursorily.

The older middle class group can, and probably should be further divided into persons of middle age (30 to 50 years) and those older. The majority of people over fifty are the ones most likely to still have faith in social immortality. They are, as is everyone else, aware of the possibility of total destruction but would tend to discount its probability. The difference between the older and younger elders can be compared to the difference between theists and agnostics. Both the theist and the person over fifty believe concretely in something. The middle aged person, like the agnostic, is not quite sure. Ambivalence about the likelihood of an extended future for society can precipitate any of three reactions: (A) Ignoring the issue from fear of confronting it. By removing the issue from quotidian concerns, one adopts a materially unnecessary present-oriented attitude toward life; and (B) committing oneself completely to working for a better future. This can be seen as a desperate attempt to create some assurance of society's continued survival, an act which in itself demands that major doubts be put aside. (C) Becoming completely disillusioned and alienated from society's problems. This analysis must remain a hypothetical construct since time and space prevent me from testing it empirically, leaving the validity of my observations unsubstantiated.

Although the following analyses must also be considered only a personal interpretation, their documentation in common knowledge and experience is more readily visible. For instance, for the elders of the ghetto, the social treadmill which has been their life experience continues to drain them of any hope for themselves and their people. For them to believe that someday "it will all be better" is as absurd as believing that our next president will be black. When Hoffman described social immortality he warned of this result. "Disillusionment comes hard in a matter such as this and is likely to lead to a change from secular to religious values out of desperation." (Feifel, p. 140). Next to death and the death-like effect of heroin, Brown's most vivid descriptions are of the religious exhibitions of his mother and her friends. Thriving religionism, with all of its ceremony, has also supported considerable business for morticians in the ghetto. But where does that leave the supposed twentieth century scientific enlightenment which eroded all faith in religious grace? In Westchester, perhaps, but not in Harlem, baby. The man-on-the-street at 125th street might think a double helix is a drink! (Who knows - maybe that is what reproduction will be like in the future.) In other words, before scientific information can undermine religious beliefs one must be aware of its implications; and before one can be aware of the implications of science one must know something about it. When you are fifty years old, strung out on dope and broke; when you have five children, no husband and a welfare check which is gone after one week; even when you are working a sixty-hour week to support your family and maybe send your son to college, scientific knowledge is not only an impossible luxury, it is irrelevant. Therefore, one could safely assume that the collective older generation living in the ghetto has not even heard the scientific arguments challenging the existence of an afterlife.

But let us suppose for the moment that these older ghetto residents had no belief in a personal afterlife. Changing only this factor, would there then be any difference in their view of death? Hoffman's theory says that, given that there is "blind faith in the linear progress toward a condition infinitely better than exists in the present" social immortality replaces personal immortality. We have already established, however, that there is no foundation for such faith in the social and economic conditions of ghetto life. This disillusionment leaves religion as the only alternative.

Interestingly enough, the attitudes of many young

middle class people (especially those stereotyped as hippies) toward life/death/future parallel those just described. They may have grown up believing in a personal afterlife; acquired knowledge refuted this faith, while at the same time predicting the inevitable improvement that future generations will enjoy as a result of our work. Many people have accepted this, believe in social immortality, live future-oriented lives, and will die futuristic deaths. However, the numbers of disillusioned young people continue to increase. With many it is not because they are merely <u>uncertain</u> about society's future existence, but because they are convinced of its inevitable, perhaps imminent destruction. This can account for the surge of interest in Eastern philosophy, numerology and mysticism, all of which are, in effect, comparable to ghetto religionism. Disillusionment taken one step further results in the dissociation of the self from any future. It is an often drugged, alienated live-for-the-moment-because-nothing-else-matters existence. It is apolitical, amoral but not atypical. Death is the end of a generally bad trip that had its moments.

In our discussion thus far we have seen that when the future after death looks uncertain, both personally and socially, people either become very alienated or turn back in frustration to religion. Young blacks in the ghetto have forged another alternative, (together with their peers of the middle class). It is especially interesting because it makes the social future contingent on personal future, and personal future depends on self-assertion now. This implies the idea that if at death one sees no future hope it is because he has not created that hope in his life. In effect, the whole black movement has gained strength because it has created its own hope and has developed its own mores around the sustenance of that hope. This very faith poses a threat to the white ruling class because its promises will be realized with or without the help or consent of any other group. It means that there is now a greater, unified cause for living. And although for the majority it will not always be so, there is also a greater cause for dying. Martin Luther King and Malcolm X died tragic deaths, but they were not without hope. In his eloquent eulogy of Malcolm X, Ossie Davis (Cleaver, 1968, p.61) expressed this hope:

> Malcolm was our manhood, our living, black manhood! This was his meaning to his people.

> And, in honoring him, we honor the best in ourselves...And we will know him then for what he was and is--a Prince--our own black shining Prince!--who didn't hesitate to die, because he loved us so.

Eldridge Cleaver picked up this torch and made it their destiny (p.61):

> We shall have our manhood. We shall have it or the earth will be leveled by our attempts to gain it.

We have established that some attitudes and concepts of death and the future that were once clearly divided according to economics and environment are changing. We have traced similarities between different age groups in and out of the ghetto. Attitudes toward death vary according to factors other than just socio-economic status, race and environment. But all of these variations rest on one primary, inescapable difference: middle class society has shunned death, ignored it, repressed it to the level of the pornographic, and if at all possible, would like to eliminate it. One gets the feeling that people are saying, "Don't call us, we'll call you." Death is not so easily co-opted in the ghetto. It is a universal neighbor, bed-partner, schoolmate.. it is a fact of life learned very early and never forgotten.

References

Brown, Claude. Manchild in the Promised Land, New York: Signet, 1965.

Bruce, Lenny. How to Talk Dirty and Influence People. Chicago: HMH Publishing Co., 1963.

Cleaver, Eldridge. Soul on Ice, New York: Dell, 1968.

Conot, Robert. Rivers of Blood, Years of Darkness, New York: Bantam, 1967.

Coser, Lewis A. "Violence and the social Structure", Violence in the Streets, S. Endleman. (Ed.)

Feifel, Herman. The Meaning of Death. New York: McGraw-Hill, 1959.

Gorer, Geoffrey. Death, Grief, and Mourning, Garden City, New York: Doubleday, 1965.

The Autobiography of Malcolm X. New York: Grove Press, 1964.

Chapter 2

Hope and Suicide in the Concentration Camp

Christopher W. Beaver

The concentration camps created by the Nazis in 1933 and maintained by them until their defeat in 1945 seem to present conditions under which the incidence of suicide should be great. After a period of general persecution and degradation, an individual would be removed to a camp. Separation of family members occurred as prisoners arrived at a camp, after being shipped under conditions which most often precluded identification of locale. The separation process was termed selection as the strongest detainees were chosen for their potential as workers. Should one be too infirm or weak for labor, immediate death was the sentence.

At some stage of one's internment it became evident with a high degree of certainty that the Nazis intended to allow no one, especially the Jews to survive the camps. Evidence of deaths by gas and other means cropped up as guards spoke to the inmates, fellow prisoners assigned to corpse disposal spoke, olfactory senses responded to the crematoria or simply by rumor or the grapevine. Efforts to prevent contact between deathworkers and other inmates invariably failed as experiences at Treblinka reveal. The camp was divided into several strictly segregated parts. One dealt exclusively with corpse disposal and the workers were themselves destroyed every three months. Still, detailed word of the activities reached the other parts of the camp. (Steiner,1967).

Thus, Jews, as a group singled out for persecution, lived in the shadow of unnatural and unaccountable death--their only crime in being Jewish. The extent and reality of this can be realized if one understands that ultimately 72 per cent of European Jewry was destroyed--six million people (Friedlander, 1968, p. 18). Other groups such as Communists and Jehovah's Witnesses underwent similar though less stringent persecutions, largely because they were less visible than the Jews. Nevertheless, three million of these people perished in the camps by 1945.

Chances for survival in the face of concerted Nazi efforts to the contrary were almost nil. Aside from the direct method of killing by one act, indirect deaths were also caused by the combination of strenuous labor and low calorie diet. Sanitation facilities were primitive and virtually nonexistent. Fatigue was an ever-existing state constantly exacerbated by interruptions of the few hours sleep generally allowed. Medical care was no more than a grisly farce. Guards continually subjected the prisoners to insult and degradation. Prisoners, separated from friends, lost supportive relationships. The individual finally lost all control of a hostile environment which operated according to no laws he had experienced or believed in.

These comments are made from my perspective, twenty-five years later. How the individuals involved responded to what may be called objective circumstances follows in the wake of an important point. Despite apparent conditions conducive to suicide, crisis situations being a prodromal aspect of suicide, there were few overt suicides in the camps. Hope is removed from the inmates' landscape (Ehrmann, 1965, p.135). One's inability to hope is a key element in suicides. Part of the inability was "a state of anxiety, fear and uncertainty about one's own fate and that of one's nearest and dearest." (Ehrmann, 1965, p.135) The burden of constant anxiety is terrible to bear. It is a state of constant uneasiness and foreboding whose object may or may not be clearly defined, but the remedy of which is beyond grasp, actual or fantasized. "The loss of present comforts . . .was not as frightening as fear of the future." (Vaughn, 1949, p.117) Combined, the above gave rise to severe depression which, although associated with suicide only slightly more than half the time, is a strong factor: and is, in any case, suggestive of camp conditions. Another reaction, cited by Cohen (1953, p.120) was acute fright. This was especially difficult to cope with for those from a relatively stable and secure status outside the camp.

Another focus is Durkheim's concept of anomie. Although questions have been raised regarding the practical validity of his constructs, anomie successfully describes the despair engendered by estrangement from interpersonal ties and a stable, applicable moral or philosophic standard. In this sense, inmates suffered from anomie and the concomitant feelings of despair and worthlessness.

It is assumed with Bettelheim (1960, p.259) that men

"can be pushed so far and no further; that beyond a certain point he chooses death to an inhuman existence." The prime assertion of the paper is that when an individual understands his position to be past that barrier and becomes aware that all hope is unfounded, suicide appears as a seductive alternative to life. However, he need not reach that stage if other mechanisms and happenstance intervene and protect him from the realization. Legions of these things exist and may be religious codes, previous acclimation to conditions of deprivation, being caught up in the struggle for survival in which nothing exists beyond the pure ego, etc. In the specialized environment of the concentration camps the working out of the assertion can be illustrated.

The idea of intention in self-destructive acts has been systematically elaborated by Shneidman into three degrees: intention, sub-intention and un-intention. The stages represent the individual's actual, not self-perceived, attitude toward causing his own death. A subintentional death would therefore include placing oneself in dangerous circumstances in order to test the judgment of fate - neglecting to take needed medicine, driving at unsafe speeds, even crossing against the light. Death is not really the object, but life's termination is possible or probable through the individual's actions. I feel more comfortable with speaking of degrees of intention and will use this useful concept to describe certain deaths in the camps.

There exist of course intentions on various levels. In discussing concentration camps the idea of levels is always present. In a sense, no deaths were self-intentional since they were imposed from without by the Nazis. Yet within this framework, choices could be made and intentional levels did exist.

One group of inmates is customarily excluded from discussion of suicidal versus nonsuicidal prisoners. These are the people whom, it is said, acquiesced in their own deaths. Cohen (p.158) quotes Bluhm, noting that, "Death in a Nazi concentration camp requires no explanation. Survival does." In the camp, no one would force another to live. ". . .The prisoners' behavior cannot be but individual. . ." writes Cohen; and individual means for him the terrifying sense of total solitariness vis-a-vis one's hostile and life-threatening environment. Hence, one could easily die by ceasing to resist the tendency of the environment. Bettelheim describes people in this group, calling them by their camp name:

> Prisoners who came to believe the repeated statements of the guards--that there was no hope for them, that they would never leave the camp except as a corpse--who came to feel that their environment was one over which they could exercise no influence whatsoever, these prisoners were, in a literal sense, walking corpses. In the camps they were called 'moslems' (Muselmanner) because of what was erroneously viewed as a fatalistic surrender to the environment, as Mohammedans are supposed to blandly accept their fate. (Bettelheim, 1960, p.151)

They carried no intention to die, they merely acquiesced in their own deaths. In the battle with Nazis for life, they had lost and were beaten men.

As death approached, the musselmen became more and more listless and unresponsive to external stimuli, gradually withdrawing from life. Despite the slow approach to death, not always was "this dying like the gradual going out of a candlelight." (Cohen, 1953, p.72) Sometimes "the 'musselman' died quite suddenly, in his sleep or perhaps at roll call." (Rosencher quoted by Cohen,p.72)

Regarding these individuals it is improper to assign any degree of intention to their deaths; although for them, life had lost all hopeful properties. Stengel tentatively terms deaths of this sort uncommon suicides, pointing out, as cited before, that "one had only to relax in the struggle for survival to succumb rapidly." (Stengel, 1964, p.110) Cohen labels the deaths of the musselmen passive suicides, but remarks that, "This for of suicide. . .eludes observation; hence no estimate of its frequency can be made, and it must be left out of account in an attempt to explain the small number of suicides." (Cohen, p.160)

In their analysis, both Stengel and Cohen err. The emphasis must be rearranged and the type of death correctly established. Friedlander eloquently states the plight of all inmates who perished and is especially revealing in this instance. He writes of the dead prisoners: "They did not all die as heroes--and we would be playing the Nazis' game if we were to demand heroism from them. They were victims." (Friedlander, p.15) Viewed through Friedlander's lens, Bettelheim's description of the guards' tauntings that there was no hope, is brought into focus. The words combined with the sensual and emotional experience, sketched above, to kill susceptible men. The most susceptible were those who previously held high status, secure positions and were shocked into over-realization of their circumstances. Over-realization meaning that the imprint was so strong, all chance of finding hope or benefitting from psychologically protective mechanisms was irrevocably lost. The victims did not surrender their lives nor seek to end their suffering; rather hope was snatched from them and they could no longer struggle for life. At this stage, they acquiesced in their deaths, but were, in a sense, forced to do so.

Bettelheim suggests that in effect, all prisoners were similar to the musselmen:

> In the extermination camps the prisoners were also deprived of anything that might have restored self-respect or the will to live, while the pent-up hostility grew uninterruptedly.
>
> All this may explain the docility of prisoners who walked to the gas chambers or who dug their own graves and then lined up before them so that, shot down, they would fall into the graves. It may be assumed that most of these prisoners were by then suicidal. . .Psychologically speaking, most prisoners in the extermination camps committed suicide by submitting to death without resistance. (Bettelheim, pp. 250-251)

As most writers commenting on suicide have realized, how one's death is categorized can have definite meaning for survivors. Bettelheim must be corrected. He underplays the nature of the camps and fails to identify the dead as victims. Another point of his is that the inmates had, many years before, cooperated in their own deaths by ignoring the nascent challenge to their lives represented by Hitler's rise. Reasons for this are to be given below. Yet regarding the groupings already mentioned it is incorrect and unfair to subsume all those who were killed under the heading sub-intentional suicide.

Were there then no suicides with intentional content? Actually, suicides did occur and four different types will be discussed.

The first set of suicides are those whose motivations result from the objective circumstances which one might expect to see. Cohen quotes Bondy: "Life in Buchenwald (during November, 1938) was so wild and unbearable that many of the inmates committed suicide by severing an artery or running into the electrically charged wire. . . It was especially bad during the first few days and nights." (Cohen, p. 124) Important are the careful time limits with which Bondy bounds his account and the specification that conditions in Buchenwald became overwhelming beyond even the usual pattern, before intentional suicides occurred. That these were intentional is established by the suicide's knowledge that little help would be extended to him and by the serious nature of the attempt. Survival could not be considered when the method chosen was the electrified wire. Other means presented only slightly less certain death.

Stengel alludes to the second suicidal class in his discussion of the camps. He notes there, the "occasional suicide epidemics," in which groups of people would overtly destroy themselves, by hanging or throwing themselves from heights such as at quarries where they labored. (Stengel, p.109) He offers no explanation for the phenomenon. In the book Treblinka, which is written in the novel format, though based on carefully researched fact, an account is given detailing one incident of epidemical suicide. As a prelude to ultimate revolt against the captors and in an effort to wrest control of their lives from the Nazis, groups of prisoners killed themselves. (Quoted from recollection) Death by Nazi will was extremely evident, because the camp was self-liquidating to an intensive degree. That is, prisoners were directed to dispose of the bodies of those gassed and they in turn were rapidly killed. There were very few long-term prisoners (more than two and a half years in the camps.)

Nehru enlightens on this point in his book, The Discovery of India. (1947). There he tells of an encounter with an older countryman. Nehru was told that man's ability to destroy himself is his sole birthright. No one can take that from him. Nehru admits to being comforted by the fact that he always preserved this last measure of autonomy. (Quoted from recollection) Weisman (1967,p.291) in concordance, notes that, "For some patients, self-destruction . . .(is a way) to 'normalize' themselves: to feel in control, not enslaved; to attain consummation not extinction; and, in effect, to be wholly responsible."

The epidemics originated in group decisions to defy the Nazis. How effective was the tactic may be judged by Bettelheim's analysis:

> The stated principle (of the Nazis) was: the more prisoners to commit suicide, the better. . . an SS man might provoke a prisoner to commit suicide. . .and that was all right. But for those who took the initiative in killing themselves, the SS issued (in Dachau in 1933) a special order: prisoners who attempted suicide but did not succeed were to receive twenty-five lashes and prolonged solitary confinement. Supposedly this was to punish them for their failure to do away with themselves; but I am convinced it was much more to punish them for the act of self-determination. (Bettelheim, pp. 150-151)

Given Bettelheim's assessment and the statement about Treblinka, the first suicides in the group take on rational attributes. Rational defined as behavior generated by realistic appraisal of one's situation. Debate may linger on whether any self-destructive act is rational; but these suicides were rational to the extent that they were appropriate for the individuals involved and would be an effective act. The latter is certified by Bettelheim. Of the former it seems that suicide may be more fitting than gassing, because it represents a refusal to accept a controlling authority and prevailing philosophy antithetical to one in its every manifestation. The suicides were obeying the logic Marcuse (1959, p.76) puts forward in his article, "The Ideology of Death." He says, "Compliance with death is compliance with the master over death." While Marcuse would argue that suicide is such compliance, in the camps it might be as rational a choice as mass revolt.

In fact, mass suicide may properly be seen to be the only choice of resistance without hope. Cohen (1953, p.166 notes that hopelessness was a factor in the group suicides. Fryd (1965, p.217) recalls the words of Karel Polacek:

> Once I saw an old Bible picture. The Antichrist was about to pierce a saint through with his lance. The saint was sitting comfortably there, as if it had nothing to do with him. Formerly I used to think that the medieval painters were incapable of presenting feelings like fear, astonishment or pain, so it looked as if the saints had shown no interest in their own

martyrdom. Now I understand the saints better: what could they do?

Again, Donat (1968, p.180) asks, "Why does the man unjustly condemned to death fail to turn on his guards as he is led to the gallows?" His answer is simple: ". . .there can be no struggle without some hope." The hopelessness of revolt overcomes all other considerations. "There is no way of winning; they have us." (Wells, 1968, p.248). In these circumstances the group suicides become understandable as a means of defiance.

Although hopelessness is stressed as the key factor in directing defiance into suicide, there are other psychological dynamics in operation. In _Suicide and Attempted Suicide,_ Stengel (1964) notes the link between aggression and suicide and he, along with others, considers some suicides redirected impulses to murder, and vice versa. Thus, in the state of hopelessness, suicide may become a surrogate for murder, that is, revolt against the Nazis.

Another feature operative is the feeling of martyrdom appearing in the minds of many prisoners. Polacek's words, making the simile between his lot and the fate of the saints, clearly partakes of this quality. Shneidman (1970) has spoken of wishing to deromanticize death. That is, he wants to divest death of its glory association--concepts such as self-sacrifice, of which martyrdom is a sub-section. These figurations refer, of course, to unnecessary death.

In the same article, Shneidman refers to the generative time of one's life, the years of old age, in which one makes great emotional investment in one's progeny. Implied in the generative period is a turning away from one's ego concerns and a focusing on one's life in others.

Shneidman attempted to convey the paucity of "cultural rationalizations" which aim at producing comfortable acceptance of untimely deaths, and which, in the extreme case, can lead people to seek out a poetic, "rationalized" demise. The idea of martyrdom has the heroic connotations which can lead to a state of resignation to one's supposed fate, but it also shares the generative quality. Combined, these result in psychological barriers blocking struggle against oppressive forces. As with Polacek, Kaplan (1968, p.189) reflects acceptance with death via a sense of martyrdom. "Among ourselves we fully admit that this death which lurks behind our walls will be our salvation." Kaplan's sense of the romanticized death is also evidenced by his comments on the death of the president of the Warsaw ghetto, Adam Czerniakow: "He did not have a good life, but he had a beautiful death. May his death atone for his wrongs against his people before becoming president." (p.191) Both men could cope with their hopeless positions by taking refuge in the moral superiority implied by the martyr's refusal to be moved by death. Rationalization of a poor position is clearly occurring, but there is more to be remarked about the generative facet of their situation.

The investment in future generations may be more than simple rationalization. The style of one's death has in fact great relevance for the values of ensuing generations. Thus, Polacek's stoic acceptance of death may, ultimately, further the philosophy in which he believed. Had the saints or Polacek striven to carry out a revolt which was abortive or offered some last resistance, undue emphasis may be placed on a desire for life, superseding their desire for a moral life. This would be more true in the case of the Jews who wish to foster a religious view of life which finds values beyond a present, bare existence.

Life as a purely generative mode also accounts for the survival of many in the camps. "One must want to survive, to bear witness. . .to remain alive, not to begin to die." (Manvell and Fraenkel, 1967, p.150) Or again, "I felt that continuing this diary to the very end of my physical and spiritual strength is a historical mission which must not be abandoned. My mind is still clear, my need to record unstilled, though it is now five days since any real food has passed my lips." (Friedlander, 1968, p. 129) Existence of this kind is generative because it grounds itself solely on others. The writer struggles to survive so future generations will hear the truth. Much can be endured in expectation, one might say, in hope, of future vindication and justice.

There are many, many, other reasons for the lack of resistance. Donat (1968, p.58) says, "What defeated us, ultimately, was Jewry's indestructible optimism, our eternal faith in the goodness of man--or rather, in the limits of his degradation." Diamant describes camp conditions which prevented organization, activity and an immediate goal, factors he believes are essential for rebellion. He then asks, "How could such a broken group of people revolt, when they were so thoroughly isolated from the rest of the population and from weapons?" (1965,p.132) One might assume much less cohesive planing is required for mass self-destruction. Bettelheim (1960, p.249) also looks to historical reasons: ". . .it must be realized that the most active individuals had long ago made their efforts to fight National Socialism and were now either dead or exhausted." Finally, Manvell and Fraenkel (1967, p.172) ascribe the explanation to Nazi policy:

> . . .everyone knew that acts of violence by prisoners against authority would inevitably lead to monstrous reprisals which affected the whole prison population; the S.S. insisted on regarding any form of rebellion, however individual, as a matter of 'collective responsibility', and for this reason alone open disobedience or violence was never encouraged by responsible elements among the prison resistance.

One final issue raised by group suicide is why groups rather than individuals destroyed themselves. Stengel (1964, p.48) broaches the subject of imitation as a factor: ". . .the urge to imitation alone is unlikely to cause anybody to take his life unless his state of mind predisposes him to such an action and unless there exists a close relationship with the person whose behavior he adopts." Hence, those who followed the first suicides might have been moved by group pressures even though part of the group was dead.

Stengel goes on to note (p.48): "Suicides of whole groups and communities are known to have occurred in times of war and persecution: they were not due to simple imitation but to a collective refusal to survive." Even beyond the negative refusal to survive, which may be doubted in the face of previous discussion, group suicide was a positive and intentioned act of defiance.

There are yet two more forms of self-extinctive behavior to discuss. One is fully related by Bettelheim (p.162):

> . . .(there were a) few prisoners who became convinced that no one could live in the camps longer than a certain number of years without changing his attitudes so radically that he could no longer be considered, or again become, the person he once

> was. Therefore they set a time limit for themselves beyond which, in their opinion, there was no point staying alive since from then on life would simply consist of being prisoners in a concentration camp. These were men who could not endure acquiring those attitudes and behaviors they saw developing in most old prisoners. They therefore set a fixed date for committing suicide. One of them set the sixth anniversary of his arrival in the camp because he felt that nobody there was worth saving after five years. His friends tried to watch him carefully on that day, but nevertheless he succeeded.

These people felt hopeless. Their world-view narrowed, a common component of self-destructive persons and they saw only two alternatives--release from camp by a certain date or death.

A final group of suicides were those caused by hunger. For Cohen (1953, p.140) hunger played such a dominant role in behavior (as a prompter, but also as a suppressor of other drives, especially the sexual) that he believed it the primary drive. Cohen says hunger effectively reduced many to absolute egoists, survival of self being their only value. Wiesel (1968, p.407) cites a suicide caused by hunger and says the individual violated what Cohen calls the reality-principle. "If this principle could permit the hunger drive to be satisfied without peril to the individual's life, it would be satisfied." (Cohen, 1953, p.158)

Deaths due to self-destructive cravings for food were therefore slightly intentional only and, of course, irrational. They were irrational in that they arose from a distortion of reality and were uncontrollable. Intention levels were low because the victim pursued a dangerous course whose object was not death, nor even a judgment from fate, but rather life, the satisfaction of hunger. Other deaths occurred when the literally hunger-crazed threw themselves on the electrified wire, not even attempting to secure food. The persons involved exhibited a state in which reality ceased to have meaning and they no longer directed their own actions. Escape from hunger was blindly sought. That it terminated in self-destruction was fortuitous.

From all this, it may be seen that hope is a key factor in determining the individual's ability to continue existence under very adverse conditions. Hope manifested itself most basically as the belief that "Whatever is terrible will pass before I do." (Hentoff, 1969)Hope defines itself in the quoted phrase as a belief that a beneficial aspiration will be fulfilled. This helps explain the almost mystical ability of prisoners to persevere. When an inmate could no longer have faith in the basic life-aspiration, the result would often be suicide.

To break down the faith, the Nazis embarked on a careful campaign of virulent anti-Semitism to raise doubts about the worthiness of the life-aspiration held by the Jewish inmates. "Racial persecution deliberately undermined and violated the fundamental conditions for a healthy mental life: self-confidence, satisfaction with one's work, the possibility of satisfying basic needs, the possibility of making free decision and of freely living one's life." (Diamant, 1965 p.129) The undertone of the Nazi statement that one would leave the camps only as a corpse is that any other thoughts are improper in the moral sense.

Many accounts paint pictures of what hope was in the camps. Diamant (p.135) writes of the creation of irrational hope as an attempt to compensate for the "loss of meaning of life." Despite the revelations of the total mass death as a certainty, many people refused to believe the words they heard. Evidence of the irrational hope lies in the words of fourteen-year-old Charlotte Veresova writing from the Terezin ghetto, a city become concentration camp. Her diary reads: "It is rumoured that they are building gas chambers here. People whisper about it and they really are building something mysterious in the fortification catacombs with airtight doors. They (the Nazis) say a duck farm. What for? Might it still be gas? I can't believe it. It is too terrible." (Terezin, p.111)

Mingled in with the irrational hope is still another strand. Disbelief. In giving another reason why Jewish resistance to the Nazis was never an armed act, Donat (1968, p.179) touches on this subject: "The basic factor in the Ghetto's lack of preparation for armed resistance was psychological; we did not at first believe the Resettlement Operation to be what in fact it was, systematic slaughter of the entire Jewish population." As long as disbelief existed the crisis situation did not reduce to a question of hope. Only when the truly existential moment occurred, when systematic extermination was seen as real, did hope, or its lack, become a dominant dynamic. Up to that stage hope did not come to the forefront or was expressed as the objective disbelief described above. Cohen (1953, p.118) admits he cherished certain delusions and repressed intelligence that did not fit.

Objective disbelief (that is, disbelief in the reality of events in the individual's external world) was fostered by the Nazis as a means of control. In the words of a Nazi official (Friedlander 1968, p.61):

> The mass of the Jewish people were taken completely by surprise. Never before has a people gone so unsuspectingly to its disaster. After the first anti-Jewish actions of the Germans, they thought now the wave was over and so they walked back to their undoing.

Another said, "One of the most giant hoaxes in world history was perpetrated on five million people noted for their intellect." (Friedlander, p.61) Commenting on this Donat says, "There is abundant evidence that Jews took at face value German assurances that it was a bona fide resettlement (rather than internment)." (Friedlander, p.61)

Another mode of subterfuge was used in the Warsaw ghetto, the effect of which was to create false hope and encourage people to cooperate with the Nazis. Various identification cards were issued to all inhabitants. The Nazis then rounded up holders of certain cards. The others played the game praying to be spared. But the rules changed and new groups of cards were issued. The parameters were never stable and shifted paratactically.

The tragedy of the ghetto stemmed, therefore, from the inhabitants' unwillingness and inability to believe that there was no rational, logical plan for continued, stable existence. They believed survival, or at least avoidance of deportation, depended on discovering the proper classification. They failed to see that the only order in the Nazi's procedure was the order of mass destruction.

Andre Schwarz-Bart, in The Last of the Just (1968), graphically depicts the transfiguration of objective disbelief to subjective disbelief (the person doesn't perceive the objective events, which are real, as happening to himself, to the ego): ". . .all these things were without precedent (the objective perception). . ." and later: "These events concerned someone else (the subjective perception)." (p.96) Both views combine in the distorted view that "Nothing like them (the events) had ever happened to anybody." (p.96)

The detachment form self is cited many times as a defense mechanism by which the ego, existing as one's mental image of oneself, is protected from shock by a hypothetical distance from one's physical presence. Manvell and Fraenkel (1967, p.159) quoting a witness at the Eichmann trial relate that:

> Without realizing it, one gradually begins to apply what is called self-hypnotism to shut off certain connections between the brain and the body. In time, one begins to witness the most brutal and degrading scenes without reacting; a person may be killed before one's eyes, and one views it without reacting too emotionally, simply records it as a machine might. The same process applies to personal beatings.

As a postscript to the discussion of hunger as a factor in suicide, the witness testified that no detachment was possible in the face of hunger. Synthesizing the process of detachment and the part of hunger, Primo Levi describes a fellow inmate: "He had a wife and five children and a prosperous business as a saddler, but for a long time now he has grown accustomed to thinking of himself only as a sack which needs periodic refilling." Man becomes one half of a dichotomous being cut off from the material, depersonalized object comprising the rest of him. The division is highly functional for the survival of the man, reducing him to a level of consciousness resistant to otherwise intolerable degradation, and yet leaving him sensitive enough to the environment to secure food and other bare essentials.

The secondary dimension to detachment from self was referred to by the witness at the Eichmann trial. One's fellow prisoners constantly died or were executed, and for many these occurrences finally lost meaning. Wiesel (1968, p.410), recounts a hanging which the whole camp was forced to observe:

> . . .the whole camp, block after block, had to march past the hanged man and stare at the dimmed

eyes, the lolling tongue of death. The Kapos and heads of each block forced everyone to look him full in the face. After the march, we were given permission to return to the blocks for our meal. I remember that I found the soup excellent that evening ..." The account is machine-like just as described by the Eichmann witness.

The detachment from self combined with acceptance of death as a natural order produced a resignation to one's own death. Wells (1968, p.248) tells of accidentally dropping a beam as a member of a work gang: "I am sure they will shoot me! But I don't care; I think: Let them get it over with." Wells own will plays no part. Death is no longer within his province. He speaks as if it will merely happen.

The final stage of the contact with frequent death is used by Cohen to help explain the persistent question, why did the prisoners not resist their captors more adamantly: "The adaptation to concentration-camp life and the residing in the 'realm of death' cause death to lose its terror, for death has become normal. This will also account for the quietness with which those prisoners who knew they were going to the gas chambers met their fate.. people as a rule will not resist the normal." (Cohen,1953, p.167)

Again the question of hope does not arise because the victims had become so numbed to their environment its dominance was complete. The pathway to the gas chambers one could not control. The inmates were no longer sensitive or resistant enough to their environment to require the sustaining power of hope. They were caught up in merely getting along.

Other explanations of the low suicide rates in concentration camps say that no dyadic relationships (involving a significant other) could exist, so suicides as appeals for sympathy were ruled out; or likewise, because the individual knew there was little chance of someone coming to his aid, suicide as a cry for help would not be considered; or finally that suicide fulfills an escape function and in the camps the only escape was to live. (Stengel, p.110) For the general drop in rates during crises, Stengel (1964, p.110) hypothesizes three explanations: "less social isolation, direction of aggressive feelings from the threatened self against the (clear and) external enemy, and decline of the value of the individual." There is some truth to each of these.

However, in the wake of the previous analysis, the attitudes represented by Stengel's explanations, and those described above, can be seen as psychological defenses called forth to cushion the individual against the extreme stresses caused by crisis, and especially the concentration camp environment. Without these protections and unless hope is generated in some manner, the individual stands a high likelihood of turning to suicide as an alternative to situations he is unable to bear.

Postscript:

As I poured over the records of the concentration camps, I felt the need to say something about them beyond the range of the study proper. But I could not find enough words. The final few sentences, therefore, are from Night and Fog, a film written by Jean Cayrol (1962) and directed by Alain Resnais:

> The crematorium is no longer in use. The devices of the Nazis are out of date. Nine million dead haunt this landscape. Who is on the lookout from this strange tower to warn us of the coming of new executioners? Are their faces really different from our own?. . .There are those of us who sincerely look upon the ruins today, as if the old concentration camp monster were dead and buried beneath them. Those who pretend to take hope again as the image fades, as though there were a cure for the plague of these camps. Those of us who pretend to believe that all this happened only once, at a certain time and in a certain place, and those who refuse to see, who do not hear the cry to the end of time.

References

Bettelheim, Bruno. The Informed Heart. Glencoe: The Free Press, 1960.

Cayrol, Jean. Night and Fog. In Robert Hughes (Ed.), Film: Book 2, Films of Peace and War. New York: Grove Press, 1962.

Cohen, Elie A. Human Behavior in the Concentration Camp. New York: W. W. Norton, 1953.

Diamant, Jiri. Some Comments on the Psychology of Life in the Ghetto Terezin. In F. Ehrmann (Ed.), Terezin. Prague: Council of Jewish Communities in the Czech Lands, 1965.

Donat, Alexander. Jewish Resistance /and/ The Holocaust Kingdom. In A. H. Friedlander (Ed.), Out of the Whirlwind. New York: Doubleday and Co., 1968.

Ehrmann, Frantisek (Ed.), Terezin. Prague: Council of Jewish Communities in the Czech Lands, 1965.

Friedlander, Albert H. (Ed.), Out of the Whirlwind. New York: Doubleday and Co., 1968.

Fryd, Norbert. Culture in the Anteroom to Hell. In F. Ehrmann (Ed.), Terezin. Prague: Council of Jewish Communities in the Czech Lands, 1965.

Gorer, Geoffrey. Death, Grief, and Mourning. New York: Anchor Books, 1965.

Hentoff, Margot. Wild Rasberries. New York Book Review, April, 1969.

Kaplan, Chaim A. The Scroll of Agony. In A. H. Friedlander (Ed.), Out of the Whirlwind. New York: Doubleday and Co., 1968.

Levi, Primo. If This is a Man. In A. H. Friedlander (Ed.), Out of the Whirlwind. New York: Doubleday and Co., 1968.

Manvell, Roger and Heinrich Fraenkel. The Incomparable Crime. New York: G. P. Putnam's Sons: 1967.

Marcuse, Herbert. The Ideology of Death. In Herman Feifel (Ed.), The Meaning of Death. New York: McGraw-Hill, 1959.

Nehru, Jawaharlal. The Discovery of India. London: Meridian Books, 1947.

Schwarz-Bart, Andre. The Last of the Just. New York: Atheneum, 1960.

Steiner, Jean Francois. Treblinka. New York: Simon and Schuster, 1967.

Stengel, Erwin. Suicide and Attempted Suicide. Baltimore: Penguin Books, 1964.

Vaughn, Elizabeth Head. Community under Stress. Princeton: Princeton University Press, 1949.

Weisman, Avery D. Self-Destruction and Sexual Perversion. In Edwin S. Shneidman (Ed.), Essays in Self-Destruction. New York: Science House, 1967.

Wells, Leon. The Jankowska Road. In A. H. Friedlander (Ed.), Out of the Whirlwind. New York: Doubleday and Co., 1968.

Wiesel, Elie. The Town beyond the Wall /and/ Night. In A. H. Friedlander (Ed.), Out of the Whirlwind. New York: Doubleday and Co., 1968.

Chapter 3

"Growing Old": Death by Installment Plan

W. F. Scoggins

> "In our theory, aging is an inevitable mutual withdrawal or disengagement, resulting in decreased interaction between the aging person and others in the social system he belongs to . . . When the aging process is complete, the equilibrium which existed in middle life between the individual and his society has given way to a new equilibrium characterized by a greater distance and an altered type of relationship. This theory is intended to apply to the aging process in all societies, although the initiation of the process may vary from culture to culture, as may the pattern of the process itself." (Cumming and Henry, 1961, pp. 14-15)

Cumming and Henry's (1961) disengagement theory proposes that a withdrawal of society from individual and individual from society occurs with age, and this process is <u>inevitable,</u> and mutually <u>satisfying.</u> Disengagement, according to Cumming and Henry, is a socio-psychobiological process. The theory is conceived in functional terms, unusual in sociology but common in anthropology. To the functionalist society constantly strives to maintain equilibrium -- to keep everything functioning well. This is antithetical to the usual symbolic-interactionist theory in social-psychology, which deals with concepts like "role changes" and "loss of roles." The functionalist assumes that both society and the individual must prepare for the potentially disruptive death of that individual, and mutual disengagement is the <u>process</u> by which this occurs. It is, according to proponents of the theory, an adjustive process, necessary for the re-establishment of the all-important equilibrium, after such disruptive events as retirement, loss of spouse, or loss of physical capabilities. Disengagement is most functional. Ultimately, disengagement prepares the individual for death and eases him out of the society which he might disrupt by dying at an inopportune time. To quote Arnold Rose (1965):

Cumming and Henry compare the disengagement of an older person to the gradual and inevitable withering of a leaf or a fruit long before frost totally kills it. This total process must be gradual, in the sense that it involves a period of preparation for death, although disengagement from some specific association or function may come suddenly. It is mutually satisfying. Society is pleased when the death of one of its members does not disrupt its ongoing functions (such as child-rearing, carrying on economic production, or the work of one of its voluntary associations). And the individual can face death with relative equanimity because he no longer has any social ties; he has said all his "goodbyes" and has nothing more to do, so he might as well "leave."

That disengagement (less interaction, fewer roles) occurs with age is an empirical observation; disengagement theory does not merely state that it occurs but proposes to explain it. Disengagement, according to Cumming and Henry, is part of the natural aging process; it occurs because it is intrinsic, because it is the natural and inevitable way that a person approaches death. Most men are "ready" to disengage before retirement occurs. Retirement is society's "permission" to men to disengage. Disengaged individuals are "free" from engaging, free from any and all obligation. Carp (1968, p.8) explicitly states that the "ability to enjoy old age may be the ability and the opportunity to use this freedom" (to disengage). The implication is that the happy elderly are disengaged, with few friends, few contacts with the world, few interests. There should be a positive association between disengagement and morale. Cumming and Henry state (p.107) that disengagement results in "an altered basis. . for the reception and initiation of social events." The old person is no longer interested in other-oriented activities, or in social events, in anything that might relate him to society (such as reading books, newspapers or material possessions). His interests turn entirely inward. Henry (1965, p.23) states that disengagement involves "a realignment of the relation of inner events to outer events in such a manner that the former take on an increasing centrality that interiority becomes increasingly important." The successful old person is the disengaged old person.

A second theory of disengagement is the reactive theory which Cumming and Henry explicitly reject. According to the reactive theory the most well-adjusted old person is the one who maintains his middle-aged (presumably high) level of engagement, i.e., who continue to be engaged in the society. One does not intrinsically lose interest with age; one loses the ability to function in society (for physical and/or social reasons). Disengagement, so supporters of this theory say, is a reaction to such losses. That is, disengagement is a negative reaction to feelings of threat, rejection or role loss. It is not satisfying. In fact, proponents would argue, the more engaged, involved and active the individual, the higher morale he would exhibit. This theory fits in neatly with overall interactionist theory; as Burgess would call it, the older person slips into the "roleless role."

The functionalist disengagement theory has a wide number of supporters (a disconcerting fact, if I may say so). The purpose of this paper is not to prove absolutely with empirical facts that this theory is wrong, but I think it is necessary to point out a few flaws in the theory. A number of investigators have attempted to test Cumming and Henry's theory. As Maddox, (1966, p.8) states: "The observed adjustment of a disengaged individual can hardly be considered to reflect an intrinsic, inevitable process in the absence of research which establishes that disengagement as a mode of adjustment is typically found even when situational constraints on the elderly person are minimal or permit alternative types of adaptation. . . in the absence of data analysis informed by a sociological perspective, it was grossly premature to advertise the behavior used to illustrate disengagement as though it represented an intrinsic, inevitable process." Havighurst, Neugarten and Tobin (1964) found that satisfaction is positively associated with social interaction among the aged. Davis (1967) found that aspiration does not decrease with age in healthy males. Lipman and Smith (1968) found that morale is positively correlated with engagement rather than disengagement, regardless of age, sex, income, health or race. Furthermore, there are serious questions about Cumming's methodology (e.g., this theory is supposedly applicable on a universal basis, but all the subjects tested were from Kansas City, Missouri). Personally, my objection lies not in the methodology, conclusions, or what have you that Cumming's arrived at during her study, but rather in the spirit of functionalist sociology and the theories it applies to explain man. They are dehumanizing. The very term "functional" implies machinery, well-oiled and robotized. Disengagement theory seems, to me, particularly insidious. The fact that such persons as Talcott Parsons ascribe to it is little short of alarming. In our post-industrial, technocratic society, "they" are trying to rob even death of its dignity, horror, emotion. Death is no longer the last enemy, to be fought and overcome, whether philosophically or medically or religiously. In our society (and every society, according to Cumming, et al) death is natural and good, a mutually satisfying contract between the individual (or, more appropriate, the masses of human beings) and the societies, the structures, that they are happening to live in. The individual naturally begins to wither, to shrink up, like an over-ripe fruit before it drops from the vine and rots. Also, in this theory, "society" takes on an overblown importance. One shrinks up emotionally, becomes inward directed, inactive, sloth-like, for the good of society. To be any other way, to live life fully, to be involved, is maladjusted. For instance, Cumming's theory would describe folk like Earl Warren, Margaret Mead, Elijah Adlow '02, Frank Boyden as maladjusted. They have insisted on remaining extremely involved in the mainstream of American life. They have refused to retire, to disinvolve, and therefore, they run the risk of disrupting society's smoothly running machine by dying. Older people should not hold important functions in a society. Society is displeased when its functions are disrupted by death. Therefore, old people are required to die, as it were, by installment plan. Little by little, every day, so that the death itself is no big thing. The final gasp of air, the cessation of awareness is really just a small step on the continuum of disengagement theory. For the older person has been slowly dying since retirement. And this is good. This is natural. This is the proper, functional way. It is efficient.

If one ascribes to Cumming's theory, then one would be appalled by the direction in which social gerontology is moving. The establishment of Golden Age Clubs, Senior Citizens Activities, the political movements started by the elderly for the elderly (e.g., the enormous support evidenced at the hearing to half MTA rates), hobby clubs etc., are efforts to re-involve the disengaged with life. A functionalist would argue, why bother. This re-engagement is potentially disruptive, and besides, the truly happy elderly are the truly useless elderly.

It is inevitable that this theory would arise in the USA. In this post-industrial era, technology has overtaken man's place in the universe. While once it was a useful tool, now man must follow it, willy-nilly, wherever it leads. Child-rearing practices, schooling, life-styles have changed radically to fit in with technological advances. College has slowly evolved from a place where one is educated, intellectually stimulated, to a training center whose graduates will supply the manpower for the technocratic society. Slowly, but inevitably, the meaning of the word "individual" is lost. The United States requires its citizens to conform; man's ideals should be society's ideals, rather than society's ideals being a sum total of the citizens ideals. And society has set itself up to propagate its goals by standardized education. The more "progress" the better. The more things produced, the more successful. And the code word is efficiency. The code word becomes youth. The elderly naturally do not fit into this. As one ages, one's efficiency is naturally decreased. Physical health eye-sight, mobility, are all naturally curtailed. Any "wisdom" one has acquired is useless; times are changing so quickly it may be inapplicable, and certainly doesn't build a better ABM. Small family units are more efficient in a technocratic society, high mobility required, so that the elderly become "chores." However, there is a bright side. If one has been depressed by the plight of the elderly, the slowly rotting elderly in the quickly moving youth-oriented USA, well, don't worry. Those retirement villages (St. Petersburg with an oxygen booth on every corner) the lonely old, the nursing homes, the elderly men in the parks, staring vacuously at nothing, the people barely eking out a living on their inadequate social securities checks, are actually being done a service by "society." By forcing retirement, the society is initiating the all-important disengagement. Lack of income is no problem. Income probably would be used for engaging enjoyments. Segregation into old age communities is a positive step, because the disengagement from society becomes even more pronounced. But the point that really bothers me is that this process is good and satisfying for the individual. It is better to die in little steps than in one big bang. The less pain, the more appropriate the method of dying. With few "goodbyes," it is easier to leave. Death, you see, is really just leaving. That is all. Death has no significance except that one more member of "society" has left. So, society must be sure that when one of its units bites the dust, it means absolutely nothing. And it also must help this unit accept death with equanimity. It sterilizes death, makes it palatable, makes it acceptable, or even attractive. This, I believe, is quite a step. To deprive death of its horror, to make an individual approach loss of self cheerfully, probably took a long time in doing. First, mandatory retirement at 65. Segregation. Minimal social security. Loss of status in families. The rationale goes, if one must die, then this is good. If one does not even care that one must die, this is better. If one has so very little to live for that one accepts death gladly, then this is the best state of affairs. The functionalist, the proponent of the disengagement theory, believes that nothing should be done to help reintegrate the elderly into society. Their talents and assets should not be used for the potentially disrupting force this would cause. The growing numbers of elderly people should gladly embrace a life of uninvolved, self-centered, disengaged, and, ultimately, extremely boring existence. After all, this prepares them for death. When death comes, you won't really care. It's time to die. Big deal. You've been almost dead for five or ten years, it's just time to cross over the line. And you've been almost dead for so long because society demands it of you, there is no place in a technocratic society for the inefficient and old. Which is too bad, but inevitable, after all, because we must pursue progress, bigger and better things, be they weapons, deodorants, or TVs. And, if you are in the way of "society's" goals, then step aside, begin to die. Try it. It's mutually satisfying.

Or so they say. I don't believe them. My sympathies lie with the symbolist-interactionists. I'm sure Dylan Thomas's did, too:

> "Do not go gently into that good night,
> Rage, rage, against the dying of the light."

References

Burgess, E. W. Aging in Western Societies. Chicago: University of Chicago Press, 1960.

Carp, F. M. (Ed.) The Retirement Process. Public Health Service Publication No. 1778. Bethesda: National Institute of Child Health and Human Development, 1968.

Cumming, E., and Henry, W.E. Growing Old: The Process of Disengagement. New York: Basic Books, 1961.

Lipman, A., and Smith K. J. Functionality of Disengagement in Old Age. Journal of Gerontology, 1968, 23, 517-525.

Rose, A. Older People and Their Social World. Philadelphia: Davis, 1965.

Chapter 4

Combat Death*

Joel Baruch

War is the professional soldier's occupation, and its prevalence upon the face of the earth since the inception of recorded time is a warm blessing to him. He does not quake convulsively at the intimation of violent death; indeed, he welcomes and pursues it. He prefers a glorious battlefield death to the ignominious demise of natural means. He believes that death without honor is the ultimate disgrace. Without the incidence of war, he is like the itinerant beggar suffering from undernourishment. War, and the death and destruction left in its wake, is insulin to his diabetic condition. In a word, he is addicted.

I know this man well because I lived with him for two years in diverse milieus- from the unbearable training camps in the United States to the desolate tropical forests of South Vietnam. I still awake suddenly during the night, sweating profusely, haunted by the memory of what I saw, and worse yet, what I did.

Stone dead, he was. Eyes wide open, staring at nothing. A thin veneer of blood curling at the corner of his lips. Two gaping holes in his chest. Right leg half gone. My first combat fatality. Violent death had raped me and usurped my virginity. A lifeless corpse where only moments before a heart beat its customary seventy pumps in one orbit of the second hand. It is one thing to hear about death; it is quite another to watch it happen. I went over to the nearest tree and vomited my guts out.

*　　　*　　　*　　　*　　　*

---

*Editor's Note: This remarkable student paper -- the one non-Harvard piece in this volume--was written for a course on Death and Suicide which I taught at U.C.L.A. in the Fall quarter of 1971. The author was in the U.S. Army from October, 1965 to September, 1967.

Combat training had never prepared me for anything like this. The death of an enemy was mentioned in aloof terms as if they were stuntmen in a cinema production, getting up and walking away after the take. With one exception, the event of your own death was never dwelled upon - rather the training period represented a world of illusions in which American soldiers seemed invulnerable to the usual etiologies of combat death.

Because the plausibility of my own extinction was so far removed from the rigors of training camp, I would fantasize frequently, conjuring up visions of self performing combat roles in heroic fashion. Ignoring all limits of personal safety, I would assault an enemy machine-gun bunker and obliterate it with hand grenades, the pins of which I had torn out with my teeth _a la_ John Wayne while moving towards the obstacle. The next sequence was an awards ceremony where I would receive a high commendation for gallantry in action -- never posthumously, but always coming through unscathed.

Fortunately, these ludicrous daydreams came to a brusque halt shortly after I was informed of my destination. Our diminutive platoon sergeant gathered us together during a bivouac exercise and stated in his normal patriarchal tone: "Men! So you will have no doubts, let it be known that you are all going to Vietnam following completion of this training course. Some of you, maybe many of you, will not be coming back. But remember! I'd rather die in the magnificence of combat than on the highways. Dying for your country is the only way to go."

A peculiar shudder invaded my body--half thrill and half fright. The culmination of my fantasies was before me in the person of this sergeant, and for the very first time, I realized that I could succumb from charging a machine-gun. A more pervasive fear of eradicating the life of another human being entered my consciousness. What gave me the right to judge whether or not my enemy should die? To this day, I thank that sergeant for contributing to my maturation.

Innovations in personality and mood are rooted in a temporal basis in a combat zone. These vicissitudes evolve in such a wily fashion that the person who is the focal point of the switch is not aware of the alteration himself. Usually, a spectacular event triggers recognition of this attitudinal mutation. That is precisely what happened to me upon observance of my second combat fatality.

Our infantry company was participating in a routine search-and-destroy mission when the staccato burst of a sniper's grease gun found its mark. Moments before I hit the ground, a trooper not more than five meters away fell over backwards as if he were struck in the face by a professional boxer. I glanced over from my prone position to see if I could help him. I couldn't because his brains were splattered everywhere, including a large chunk on the arm of my fatigue shirt. Later, after helping the medics wrap his body and load it into the plastic-canvas bag, I settled beneath a tree to meditate on the phenomenon that had just transpired.

"God, it was only a short time ago that I viewed my first dead body, and the grotesqueness of the scene made me retch uncontrollably. Now, another human being is dead, and although I'm certainly distressed and moved by what occurred, it simply doesn't affect me in the same adverse way that the first one did. His death brings feelings of sorrow, but the same misery and depression is absent. Why should I be so callous?"

"That was close! So close that I could hear the unmistakable twang of the bullets followed by the dull, empty thud that accompanies a direct hit. It could have been me just as easily. But why wasn't it? Perhaps, I am luckierthan most. I don't really think it can happen to me. When I finally expire, I will be eighty years old, lying in bed with a heroin syringe protruding from my veins."

These recapitulations of my perceptions of death, both introspective other and introspective self, announced a new dimension in my personality. That is, I was becoming impervious to the death of my fellow soldiers, and, in addition, negating the possibility of my own possible demise. Perhaps, the Freudian defense mechanism of repression was responsible--to admit these gruesome experiences to my conscious psyche might rupture the limits of my mental endurance and, thereby, induce a nervous collapse.

General Patton once remarked that "No one ever won a war by dying for his country; he makes the other bastard die for his." This statement presupposes that life is an extremely valuable commodity in a combat zone--that Pyrrhic victories are undesirable. It seems to me, however, and it did during my combat venture, that the American military command consider their troops to be less than human. We were treated as if we were inanimate objects, as fuel for the war machine or cannon fodder. Whenever a member of the American general staff was interviewed as to his principal anxiety on the contingencies of war, he would, more often than not, state the tremendous cost in human lives. Some military supervisors probably believe this. Yet I am skeptical about high-ranking officers who are expediently prompted for the unenviable job of sending men to their death and who, in a complete reversal, expound their negative feelings towards the very act that they are trained for. I once eavesdropped on a conversation between a major and a lieutenant colonel: "I hope the war doesn't end before I have another chance to earn a higher rank by serving a second tour of duty."

This type of perversion which denies the value of human life foments a cynical attitude toward the objectives of America's military institution. Promotions through the military chain of command are difficult to obtain, and in peacetime, advancements are arduous to achieve at all. Thus, the career officer who ambitiously pursues his profession needs combat action in order to ascend the military hierarchy in a hasty manner. War is an opportunity to him, and he cannot, by necessity, be overly concerned with the expenditure of precious lives. Then, too, as an officer and a more treasured piece of government property, he is seldom in the midst of the lethal combat zones where his own existence would be up for grabs. Instead, his position entitles him to dispatch low-ranking soldiers to their death.

The irreverence for human life, personified both by those in command authority and those in the ranks, is profoundly exemplified in the area of combat atrocities. As an adolescent, I had internalized the confabulations involving cruel behavior on the part of foreign enemies, or as in the case of television westerns, the insidious tactics of a band of warring Indians. But the "good guys" would never scalp and rape Indian squaws or drive elongated, wooden splinters under the thumbnail of captured prisoners of war. For they were the heroes, and they wore white costumes symbolizing their purity and goodness. Having been an attractive subject for pro-American propaganda and naive in the subtleties of human nature, I genuinely believed that pristine tortures were a part of only the enemy's game plan.

On the day of my rude awakening, our weapons platoon was to ensure that the proximous hamlet of Cu Chi was not a clandenstine haven for Viet Cong recruits. As we approached the outskirts of the village, we took cover and observed the hum-drum activity of the farmers in the surrounding rice paddies. No weapon-bearers were detected, so we warily ambled into the hamlet where the village chieftain greeted us in an amicable manner. He could speak broken English sufficiently enough to be comprehended, and without the aid of an interpreter, our platoon leader asked him where the Cong were. The chieftain denied any association with the enemy, and to this inappropriate response, the sergeant grasped the lapels of his smock and slapped him repeatedly back and forth across the face. Then, he demanded to interrogate any two men that the chieftain could find at work in the fields. The terrified village head did as ordered and returned with two young boys--no more than 15 or 16 years old. Using the old man as an interloper, the sergeant queried the boys as to their political and military affiliations. "Are you V.C.?" "Where's your next ambush?" "What are you gooks doing in this area?"

It was quite apparent that the two "suspects" were either tongue-tied out of pure fear or did not saavy what was transpiring. They couldn't answer, and the sergeant leveled the M-16 rifle he was toting at their abdominal area. As their eyes widened to a sizeable proportion, the burst of gunfire almost tore them in half. The sergeant, quite nonplussed, removed his gleaming machete from the sheath strapped to his thigh, and in two clean motions, chopped off their heads at the neck. Then, in monster-like fashion, he picked up the two heads still dripping with blood, one under each arm, and set them atop the hamlet's wooden picket fence. He lit two cigarettes and placed them in their mouths. As the remainder of the inhabitants incredulously gazed at the scene, the sergeant admonished the chieftain that if his village consorted with the Viet Cong henceforth, more incidents like the foregoing would occur. "I will behead the entire village if I have to!" We departed as the chieftain furiously nodded his assent.

In a separate encounter, I witnessed the gross differences in the burial of Viet Cong "killed-in-actions" and American dead. When an unusually large amount of the enemy were decimated in a military operation, a huge trench was dug, and the Viet Cong corpses were carelessly tossed into the ditch. The affair was reminiscent of the infamous German concentration camp illustration in which layers of decaying human bodies were cast into a gigantic crater. If some of the gung-ho "rednecks" in the outfit were assigned to burial detail, they would often make a game of it by desecrating the lifeless bodies of the enemy. The American soldier who could invent the most imaginative and outrageous sacrilege would receive the "ears of his choice". In order to win this most sought-after prize, contestants would perform such licentious tricks as placing their penis into the open mouth of a corpse or, for variety's sake, insert it into the dead man's anal orifice.

In a total antithesis, the "burial" of American dead is a somber affair. It is not a genuine burial, but a facsimile of one. The dead soldier or his dismembered parts, if they can be located, are swathed in a bag that is sent stateside for appropriate burial. American flags are cloaked around the body as if to reassure the grief-stricken survivors that he was the epitome of manhood because he perished defending freedom and democracy. Instead of the familiar desecration of corpses, a tranquil calm presides over the unceremonious duty of "burying" American troops.

Non-initiates in combat might question the authenticity of massacre reports, as I once would have, that involve "civilized" American soldiers as the willing perpetrators of such deviant acts--for it is common knowledge that American citizens are incessantly conditioned to believe that snuffing out the life energies of another human being for any reason other than self-defense is both legally and morally repugnant. It is erroneous to assume, however, that Americans with their more sophisticated approaches to life situations are incapable of such perfidy. I surmise that, at least, ninety-five per cent of the American populace has heard about the My Lai massacre in 1968. The resultant murder trials of First Lieutenant William Calley and Captain Ernest Medina functioned, inadvertently, as publicity mediums for the atrocities committed at My Lai. Disappointingly, these trials overshadowed what should have been the primary issue--that is, war creates ghouls from ordinary human beings, and it spawns unwelcome violent death.

Many individuals feel that Calley was a scapegoat in the matter because he was the only person convicted of his crimes (wantonly murdering twenty-two innocent women and children). Although I agree with this synthesis, he, nevertheless, could have refused the alleged imperatives of Captain Medina "to do away with everything" in the village both because it was illegal under the Geneva Convention of 1954 and because it countermanded the coaxings of his conscience. He did not choose these alternatives, however, and therefore, was to blame for his part in the holocaust.

The mistake was made when justice was not carried out to its logical conclusion. Indictments for murder should not have ceased with Captain Medina, but should have continued upward through the chain of command until President Nixon and former President Johnson were served notice that they, too, must share responsibility. Ultimately, the whole of American society should be indicted for its failure to insist on the termination of all wars for all time.

The American masses, for the most part, are wholly ignorant about the various nuances pertaining to the Vietnam War. Their support or displeasure for American involvement directly parallels the weekly casualty statistics in their local newspapers. A high figure elicits cries of indignation, and a lower figure evokes either stringent support or apathy. If they were only aware of the duplicity involved in the compilation of those statistics, then, perhaps, American participation in Vietnam would already be a circumstance of history.

In the first place, a major proportion of American war deaths and incapacitating injuries are external to combat. Most soldiers do not expire as a result of shrapnel wounds from hidden booby traps or land mines. Nor do most soldiers that "make" the weekly casualty lists die from injuries incurred in direct confrontation with the enemy. Rather most of the American deaths in a combat zone are attributable to the recklessness of their own personnel. I witnessed several instances of such rash behavior during my Vietnam experience. One of these, in particular, stands out in my mind.

On a humid afternoon, two members of my company were enjoying an unauthorized respite from their duties by playing catch with a live hand grenade. As they foolishly hurled the missile back and forth between them, the pin somehow came loose and tumbled to the ground, thus activating the grenade. From a distance, I heard the tremendous cacophony of the explosions, and I dropped the sandbag I was filling and rushed to the scene. A cursory glance was sufficient to reconstruct what had happened.

One of the two men was an M-79 grenadier, and at the time of the mishap, he was laden with two pouches replete with ammunition for his weapon. Unaware that the pin of the grenade that they were throwing had fallen out, he caught it just as it detonated. From this point on, the blast and its ramifications increased geometrically--his M-79 ammo exploded which, in turn, triggered the volatile Claymore mines that were protecting the perimeter of the base camp. The cylindrical steel pellets of this lethal weapon had peppered a group of soldiers laying columns of barbwire, and of the ones still alive, they were a moaning lot. A subsequent body count turned up the incredulous figure of fifteen dead and thirty-two injured.

Undoubtedly, the survivors of the dead received an official telegram from the federal government stating that their relative "died from injuries inflicted in combat." Everyone concerned, therefore, was appeased--the bereaved survivors because they possessed a piece of paper signifying the sacrifice of their beloved kin; and the powers in the governmental hierarchy because they mollified adverse reactions to their Vietnam involvement by stretching the truth.

* * * * * *

Acts of heroism are not without substantiation in any combat encounter. They do occur, perhaps not as frequently as the paperback war novel from the corner drugstore would lead one to believe. A number of Congressional Medal of Honors, the nation's supreme military award, have been given to veterans of the Vietnam conflict. Since a sizeable amount of these commendations were given to the soldier's widow or family, it is evident that one does not earn the "honor" for a trifling effort.

One of the initial medal of honors to be awarded to a Vietnam veteran went to Sergeant Daniel Fernandez, who was cited for "bravery over, above, and beyond the call of duty" because he disdained his own personal safety to save his squad members from imminent death by covering an enemy hand grenade with his body. It is interesting to cogitate the almost infinite possibilities inherent in a circumstance likethe Fernandez case. What transpired in his thoughts during the infinitesimal time that he had to realize his decision and implement it? Was it a reflex action or did he actually say to himself, "Most of us will die anyway if I don't fall on it, so why should we all perish?" And, if he had made the decision to commit a Durkheimian altruistic suicide, did he have a reversal of heart after it was already too late?

On the other side of the spectrum, what forces interact to make a man exhibit cowardly behavior? For every Daniel Fernandez, there are, I bet, ten John Does who would have made the opposite decision. Consider, for example, the non-combat situation of the notorious Kitty Genovese murder in New York where no less than thirty-seven witnesses could have intervened and possibly saved her life, yet not even one of them called the police. The situations are hardly comparable, though, when observed on a lethal perspective: Daniel Fernandez knew his chances (maybe he knew) were extremely remote that the grenade was a dud. His impending death was never really in doubt. But any one of the Genovese witnesses might have stepped in and stopped the wanton slaying without, quite possibly, suffering a mortal wound from the would-be killer's knife. Maybe the killer would have fled if someone had come to her aid. One thing is fairly certain--Daniel Fernandez would more likely have wished to tangle with the Genovese assailant rather than that cold, impersonal device.

During my tour of duty in the tropical jungles of Southeast Asia, I observed a few illustrations of outright heroism and a multitude of demonstrations of disconcerting cowardice. Moreover, I experienced both situations myself, and from those encounters, I received an invaluable lesson both in human foibles and human dignity. If some of my internalized experiences can be generalized to other soldiers trapped in similar situations (and I think they can be), then a framework for comparative perspectives is already provided. Judging from my soul-searching discourses with others in the same combat zone, I know that most possessed an uncanny desire for survival, and, at the same time, were hesitant to annihilate the enemy. Of course, there were the dissenters, a substantial minority of them--the rabble-rousers, the hatemongers, the professional soldiers--a group of men who actually relished the idea of staking their lives against those of the enemy in a contest to the death. I know this much--they were a different breed of animal.

PART II

COMMUNITY STUDIES RELATING TO DEATH AND SUICIDE

Chapter 5

Help Wanted: A Limited Study of Responses To One Person's Cry For Help

Leland Moss

M 21 STUDT GIVES SELF 3
WKS BEFORE POPPING PILLS
FOR SUICIDE. IF YOU KNOW
GOOD REASONS WHY I SHOULDN'T
PLEASE WRITE BOX D-673

It was one evening in mid-March when a group of friends and I were sitting on the edges of sanity in a place fondly known by few as The Bick; we were discussing the disparity of style and content (subjects conventionally assumed to be the domain of English majors, which we were) in issues of the _Los Angeles Free Press_ and _Boston After Dark_ (B.A.D.) classified ad sections. We got to theorizing how one juicy ad snuck in among the relatively chaste pleas in the "Personals" column might encourage other filth-ridden freaks to submit their two-cents'-worth. Alas and alack, the high price of three or four lines quickly dispelled thoughts from our nasty little heads and we jollied on drinking our gunk and chewing our gook.

Gunk and gook are not known to be conducive towards creative thinking; as a matter of fact, most fools who partake of those two famous Bick specialties quickly succumb to three ayem drowsies and plunk on home to bed. But dreams of sugar plums danced in my head and my neurons suffered a short circuit: I connected the idea of weird personals with an equally weird course on death I was taking. Wouldn't it be interesting to see how many people would respond to a call for help in a column usually devoted to undoubtedly straight and homely boys and girls blindly groping for each other? What a fascinating idea, and how easy to get out of writing the usual warmed-over garbage about My Favorite Playwright's Views Toward X (to be filled in by the appropriate subject).

As Thomas Pynchon's characters are wont to say, ha ha. For as soon as I placed my innocent little ad in B.A.D., I unleashed a torrent of sympathetic responses which drowned me in my own chicken broth. Panic. I had expected ten, maybe twenty, letters of advice regarding my suicidal plea; in the first month I received 169 letters although the ad only ran for two weeks. What to do? My original intent was to see if Shneidman's instructions to suicide prevention volunteers would be considered "common sense" by "the public" or if it would take a really dumb person to louse up a call to a center (like one of the girls heard on the record played in class). But obviously the little experiment had blossomed into a full-scale "study." Not being a social relations major (although from the vantage point of being a senior, I wish I had chosen that field), I am certainly not qualified to code all the data that can be found in these letters; therefore, what follows here is only a suggestion of what can be done with the findings. It is highly unscientific, only barely methodical, and most definitely haphazard: as I re-read each letter for its basic points, I would pay more attention to some ideas rather than others, and categories would be created and then slowly forgotten as days drifted by.

My procedure was as follows: I read each letter once, many of them quickly in the first delirium of receiving almost one hundred at my first visit to the B.A.D. mail desk. Then I began to type up notes about each letter, numbering them as I went along. The first line would contain the easily-coded information: postmark date; postmark place; sex of writer (if discernible in content of letter or by name); age of writer (if specified); and how the letter was signed. Following this, I proceeded to read the letter as carefully as possible and listed in as brief a manner as possible what the contents were. Naturally as I ploughed through the stack certain familiar phrases emerged and these were easier to code. But still, the procedure was long and occasionally painstaking and I am sure certain qualities of the letters have been overshadowed by others. After I finished this basic work, I re-read all the notes and tried to draw up categories for the ideas stated in the letters; obviously, these were for the most part arbitrary, and unfortunately it was not until half-way through this process that Shneidman mentioned the interesting differences between male and female responses on the questionnaire, so that I can only deal in the most general terms with these differences as seen in my letters.

Perhaps I should devote a few lines to the wording of the ad. It read, "M 21 studt gives self 3 wks before popping pills for suicide. If you know good reasons why I shouldn't please write Box D-673." In the first week, the two ads on either side read, "Girl who played my Flugel by Charles please call 734-3247" and "Grad Stu 26 seeks attrac Lissome well read F int'd in theatre mts shore Box D-663" -- and the two ads neighboring mine on the following week had similar slants. So much for interesting info that has almost no relevance. It is truly unfortunate, but I must honestly say that I spent very little time and thought into how my advertisement should be worded. The ads were expensive, so I tried to limit myself as much as possible, since I didn't expect a large return; it was also due to that factor that I ran the ad for two weeks. Originally I had planned to give myself a month before "popping the pills" but that became too expensive a proposition, and a week was lopped off.

It never crossed my mind to don a different persona from my own for the ad's sake. I could have said F 19 or M 34 and very probably would have received a totally different sample, but the "M 21 studt" was the first thing that occurred to me and never changed. The part about "gives self 3 weks" took more thought, since I felt the very definite need to set a time-limit on my proposed suicide for two reasons: (a) to put a limit on the date I could expect mail to come in, and (b) to create the notion that I was very serious about my intent by seeming so coldly rational about it. Putting a three-week deadline on my life implied to me at least that I had rationally decided that I alone could not find any reason to continue my existence and that rationally I was asking anyone else if they had reasons I might have overlooked. In other words, I was attempting to rule out the possibility of people hypothesizing that the ad was a joke or a threat to a girl who had walked out or any highly emotional spur-of-the-moment gesture. Why I used the word "popping" instead of "ingesting" or simply "taking" is still a question for me; perhaps I had a vague idea that "popping" would imply a rather hip frame of mind. Too, the word is somehow lighter than any others, accenting the rational quality I was trying to put across. Undoubtedly if almost any of the words in the first sentence of the ad had been different, the responses would have been altered proportionately. How many people would have tried to help an F 54 or an M 68? How many people would have decided not to write if the ad had read "before jumping off bridge" or "before slitting wrists"? These questions are unanswerable by this project, but are certainly tantalizing.

To the statistics! The females outnumbered the males by more than 2½:1, since 86 women responded as opposed to 32 men. Forty-eight of the letters were designated Unknown, since they bore no signature or reference to the writer within the body of the correspondence. It was a temptation to list most of the unknowns as female, primarily because of their handwriting, until I came upon an obviously feminine letter which turned out to be from a man when I read the signature! But another reason to classify the unsigned letters as from women is that these people would have more to lose by revealing their identities than any men, for considering the average tenor of advertisements in the personals column, girls would have many reasons to suspect that my ad was a snazzy and dramatic way to attract kooky females. In fact, quite a few girls interpreted the ad in this manner, and replied in ways similar to this response from a Mt. Holyoke student: "I think that you're just an exhibitionist that's looking for kicks -- or for some crazy young female to write back to you. You know what? It worked." (#154) On the other hand, I received no propositions from men, even though two men did refer obliquely to homosexuality; it is interesting to speculate how different things would have been had I been an "F 21" instead.

There were only one or two palpable findings upon breaking down the letters by their postmarks. As far as the postmark date is concerned, I wonder about the validity of projecting any theories at all from the statistics found, since we have no way of knowing when the writers received their copies of <u>B.A.D.</u> If we knew for certain that everyone had received his in his mailbox on April 9 and April 16, the results would be more easy to decipher, since those letters postmarked April 9 and 10 or April 16 and 17 could be deemed most "eager" to find me. But since <u>B.A.D.</u> is not a daily paper, and since the way it is distributed is widely variant, the results of the tabulation of postmark dates are highly inconclusive. Twenty-six letters bore the date of April 10 and eighteen of April 9 (and many of these had the previous day's date written on the letter proper), which does prove that quite a few of the people responded as quickly as they could. The third highest date was, strangely, April 18, which means either that those reading the ad in its second week took more time to think out their replies -- or that B.A.D. was held up by something. Three letters had no postmark, two of them having been hand-delivered while the third had a stamp but seemed to have been overlooked by the post office.

As for the postmark places, the Boston area led by a wide margin. (However, this again is misleading, for I found many letters postmarked Boston while the return address listed a suburb such as Cambridge, Watertown, Brookline,Somerville, etc. In such a case I listed the letter as coming from that suburb, but undoubtedly more letters came from places outside the central Boston area than can be traced. As it now stands, however, 88 letters apparently were mailed in Boston, as opposed to 17 in Cambridge, 8 in Amherst, 5 in Salem, 4 in Springfield (Mass.) and Providence, R.I. -- and the rest (three or less) sounds like a Boston telephone directory: Dorchester, Brighton, Medford, Andover, South Hadley, Waltham, Somerville, Brookline, Dedham, Southampton, Newton, Wellesley, Norton, Norwood, Needham Heights, Lynn, Beverly, Bedford, Auburndale, New Bedford, Quincy and Watertown). Five letters came from somewhere in New York (West N.Y., Port Washington, Poughkeepsie, Rochester and N.Y.C.) and then there were a few from places farther away than that: Appleton, Wisconsin; Louisville, Kentucky; and Rio de Janeiro, Brazil. This last, by way of explanation, came from the father of an MIT student who sent the man the ad, thinking that his father (a minister) might be able to answer better than a student.

As an interesting sideline, all of the responses were letters of the usual variety of envelopes and stationery, except for five postcards and one large package which contained an amazing amount of little goodies along with the usual poetry and hand-written sentiments.

The tabulation of the types of signatures is probably the most significant, since it involves a minimum of hypothetical judgment; it is very difficult, if not impossible, to misread a signature. I was surprised by the fact that when all the letters were classified, the largest number not only had some sort of signature, but that they were of the "full name and address" variety. As opposed to 39 of that sort, 29 letters had no signature at all (and no return address on the envelope) and 23 people signed only their first name, leaving no way to contact them except perhaps by an ad in B.A.D. (i.e., "Dear_____,please meet me at____. Box D-673"). Following these classifications, the next highest involved 20 letters which included full name, full address and a phone number; then 13 letters signed with a first name only and a phone; then 11 with first name only and an address. After this, eight letters had only an address, while three groups of four letters each had signatures of either initials only, initials and an address, or first name only, full address and phone number. Only two people left their full name and phone, while only one apiece left either only his first initial, his initials and a phone, or his full name only.

How to organize these findings? To me, the most sincere replies might be considered those who include a phone number, since that is certainly the quickest way someone in danger could contact help. All told, 40 people left their phone number along with some form of name (no one left only a phone number). This is almost 25% of the total sample and I think it is quite an astounding figure, considered where the ad was placed and in what context it was found. What these people would have said had I called them (an idea which was voted down as soon as I thought of it) is impossible to conjecture; but the simple fact that 40 people cared enough about a totally unknown 21-year-old male student to offer their help is amazing, and if I had been contemplating suicide, such a show of concern would have had to affect me in a positive manner. On a quick re-check putting the men against the women, although my figures differed in totals (I somehow arrived at 38 replies with phones instead of 40), the women outnumbered the men by 24 to 13 with one reply being either male or female (the letter is signed "Pat"). This is a ratio of approximately 1.85:1, not the same as the 2.5:1 ratio of the over-all totals. One reason for this may be the already stated notion that women would have more to lose; yet on the whole, the men's letters were much more straightforward and to the point than the others. There also seemed to be only one or two replies from men in junior colleges, as opposed to at least ten or fifteen from girls at the same education level.

When all the responses which gave some means of contacting the writer are totaled, the results come to 102, a figure which is more than half of the entire sample. This is indeed significant, especially when it is readily assumed that at the most one or two replies came from students taking Shneidman's course, a fact that can only be theorized since no one stated the fact and only a few letters came from the Cambridge area. Although a few letters had graduate Harvard dorms as return addresses, none of the letters which can be traced came from undergraduate dwellings at either Harvard or Radcliffe. (This in itself is an interesting statistic; one of the most fascinating things about the whole study was the responses I received from friends and acquaintances when I told them about my experiment. Some said they "knew" the ad was a put-on when they read it the first time; others had no idea it was fake but didn't know what to write back.) It would be valuable to discover how many of the responses did come from the more prestigious schools around the Boston area. Forty-four letters could be classified as definitely written by students of some sort, but only a few came from MIT, Harvard, Brandeis and Tufts combined. Although I have no proof, I am inclined to say that more letters came from Boston University girls than most other schools; in any case, all five of the letters from Salem came from Salem State College and all 8 issuing from Amherst came from either the major college there or University of Massachusetts at Amherst. It is tempting to say that the less "intelligent" the person, the more probable he or she will answer an ad of this sort, but the reasons for this statement are vague (e.g., they have less control over their emotions, they are more gullible (!), they have less responsibility, they have no campus riots, etc., etc.)

Contents ahoy! This was understandably the most difficult part of the whole study, and something which will probably keep a few people going much longer after this paper has been read and graded. After having read all the mail, I had some vague ideas about how to categorize what most of the people gave as "reasons why I shouldn't" and also simply what most of them said. As I re-read my summaries of each letter, however, these categories emerged and faded away between number one and one hundred sixty-nine; therefore, some of my compilations are sketchy to the point of being laughable, while others are on sturdier ground.

One of the few basic patterns of the letters was the statement, "I've felt the same way" or "I've been there, too," i.e., expressions of recognition intended to express compassion and identification, I counted 47 letters which had this type of tactic somewhere in the body of the correspondence, with three of these stating that he or she had not only been there, but had attempted suicide and failed. Perhaps the most tragic of all of these responses was the unknown person who wrote, "I've contemplated it. Eventually I did it -- committed suicide -- here in Cambridge. It was a matter of killing certain sensitivities, burning them out. . .I'm still committing suicide. Everyday I do it so that I may live." (#159) Here is an example not only of an attempt to establish camaraderie, but also of an attempt to let out one's own pain and frustration and trouble. Which brings me to the first major finding of the study, that quite a substantial amount of people responded to my cry for help with their own cry. At times this was thinly disguised as an attempt to show me I was not alone, but the person would go into so much detail about his or her past experiences that the letter became incredibly self-indulgent and eventually embarrassing. One woman wrote a fifteen-page handwritten letter (the longest I received) which spoke almost entirely about her own problems with boy friends, abortions, and doctoral exams. A student, and admittedly foreign, she was one of three people who sent me more than one letter; her second was quite frenzied and written on different sheets of paper on different days, ending up by finally giving me her phone number, which could be interpreted as a gesture antithetical to all that preceded. This letter could probably be termed as the most complex received, but many others are equally difficult to judge as to their basic function -- as a catharsis for the writer or response to the addressee. Obviously, it is not necessary to rule out a double-function; but it is interesting to note that while some people termed suicide an act of supreme self-love, it has also been termed "a cry for help," and the letters acting in answer to my cry contained both aspects in heavy doses.

Another form of the self-directed letter which is not very far from the true confessions variety is the type of response wherein the writer feels he or she must explain (or simply state) that the act of writing gave him or her a sense of well-being. It is to be assumed that a large percentage of the writers did not write grudgingly but with compassion and concern, yet not very many felt an obligation to underline this. One example is this Boston girl's closing remarks: "After writing this I'd be embarrassed if you knew who I was. Well anyhow -- thank's (sic) for making me feel happy inside tonight because you made me feel for you."(#16) Of this slightly different yet similar reply, also from a girl: "I'm writing this as much for myself as for you -- I want to be a psychiatric social worker -- and <u>YOU</u> certainly sound like a challenge." (#109) While these two women were blatantly outspoken about part of the reasons they decided to answer, I am sure many more clues to this reaction can be discovered in other letters. People saw a chance to gain something by answering, either something as fleeting as a good feeling or hopefully something more palpable like a case study. Both of these responses turned me off as a reader; if I had been serious, I think I would have been terribly depressed by such responses since it would only point up the inherently mercenary quality in all relationships. (I'm talking now as if I were in a depressed state of mind).

There were other, less negative reasons as to why people responded. One nineteen-year-old Boston girl started out her letter asking "Do you know what you've done? You've demanded something of me as a human being and I don't seem to have very much -- if anything --to give you" (#107) and another stated the problem more simply by saying, "I felt a moral obligation to write to you." (#108) In other words, there were a sizable amount of people who apparently agree with Shneidman's doctrine that all suicides should be prevented, that a cry for help should be answered as swiftly and as directly as possible. Yet probably the most realistic views were these from an Amherst and a Salem girl, respectively: ". . . I have to know people need me . . . so you would be helping me as much as I would like to help you (if I responded)" (#65) and "I don't mean to talk about myself but it's the only way I can relate your emotions (sic)" (#4). In the latter, the confessional aspect of some of the letters is moderated by the reasonable objection that since the writers know very little about the potential suicide, they must resort to talking about themselves. And the former quote moderates the mercenary aspects of some other responses, by conjecturing the probably true notion that help is a two-way process.

But to return to the coding. My second highest category included all references to that rather amorphous subject known as Nature. Forty-three people listed some sort of natural occurrence as a reason to remain alive; boiled down to the essentials, what they were saying was, "It's Spring and you can't kill yourself because everything else is coming alive!" No doubt if it had been November, these same people would have asked me to wait until the thaw, so that my faith in life might be renewed. It seems that this reliance on Nature as a support for anti-suicidal views is indicative of the general notion that less suicides are committed in the spring than in any other time of the year, a notion that is apparently quite untrue, e.g. this Salem girl's statement, "You just can't die. It's not the right season" (#1). References to Nature ran the full gamut of suggestions I go to the beach and look at the beauty there to sending me a packet of morning glory seeds with instructions on how to plant them and watch them grow (#110) to the more realistic qualifications that follow paeans to life, e.g. "I could say to you, you should not commit suicide because life is too beautiful. I derive joy out of trivial things like the sun on my face, or even my daily ride on the MBTA. But that is much too subjective. Just because I enjoy flowers and springtime does not mean you do, or should." (#30) Perhaps not surprisingly, only one person mentioned a negative aspect of Nature in connection with death (I don't consider rain or unsunny days to be negative): a Boston girl informs me that "dying is painful" and then proceeds to warn me that if I commit suicide and am buried, worms will eat my body (#117). The fact that she is a tiny minority of one (and almost immediately after her warning she counters with the joys of Nature) is indicative of the sample as a whole: most of the writers are loath to mention any negative sides of life, whether it be worm-eaten corpses or Vietnam. It is indeed strange that very few people even mention the draft as a possible reason for my cry for help; I can only remember the previously mentioned foreign woman's suggestion that I write to Mrs. Nixon explaining my anti-militarist views and the Brazilian minister who specifically mentioned Vietnam as an unfortunate calamity of modern life. A larger group of people did speak in general terms of how one must take the bad with the good (cf. Avery Weisman's "I am so appalled by man's unending search for and genius for destruction, especially for destruction of his own humanity. . ." (#122) but for the most part chose to emphasize life as a good thing composed of sunny days, shining beaches, and appetizing girls. Whether this is an adequate way to fight self-destructive tendencies is debatable, but according to this sample a sizable amount of people are eager to enlist the positive forces of Nature on their side. Perhaps it is a natural human instinct to polarize subjects (good vs evil, love vs hate) and since death to most people is Nature's most negative force, it would be only human to summon up positive natural forces against it.

Following close on the heels of Nature as a recurrent theme was doubting and mistrusting. Thirty-eight people boldly stated that they were not sure if the ad was for real, yet proceeded to treat the cry as if it were quite genuine. Undoubtedly this mistrust was one of the first things that came to their minds, since it was either placed at the beginning or end of the letters, hardly ever in the middle as an afterthought. There is good reason to expect this sort of reaction, considering where the ad was found, but it seems strange that so many people felt obliged to protect their self-esteem by announcing that if it is all a joke, they weren't taken. Quite a shaky basis on which to approach a potential suicide! Many letters started almost immediately with this typical phrase: "I presume you're serious, if you're not, it's a bad joke" (#6) Anxiety about the possibility of being put-on reached a climax with this postscript from a Dorchester man, "If this is a joke or hoax you owe me a six cent stamp and deserve to be murdered!!" (#85). But even though this last response is obviously an over-reaction, it probably makes evident what many more inhibited people actually feel about treating suicide as a joke; it is as if I were insulting their basic humanity by laughing at their concern for human life. However, the most healthy and probably most normal response was beautifully stated by this person: "At first I wondered if you were serious or not and I admit I still wonder. Then I decided that if it is a joke, its in poor taste, the joke's on me, and I don't care. If you're serious, I'd have the apathy more on my conscience for not writing" (#3). It was assuredly the worry about apathy which led the others to write in as well, even though the whole thing may have been (and was) a trap.

A smaller yet still substantial number of people used their doubts in a more constructive manner by writing that the fact that I placed the ad in <u>B.A.D.</u>

proves that I'm not really serious. While these people may have doubted the whole idea at first glance, it is obvious that they thought longer about the negative side-effects of telling someone who very well may be a potential suicide that they don't believe in him; these writers turned their misgivings wholly onto the addressee's shoulders by not doubting his intention as a cry for help but by analyzing the intention itself as a reason to stay alive. To them, the fact that a person is still looking for help should be reason enough for him to avoid suicide: ". . .you obviously want to live, or you wouldn't have put the ad in the paper" (#2).

Carrying the sentiment expressed in the last quote one step further is to show that a cry for help is an other-oriented action, a last reach for one other person to grab and take hold. What those people were doing when they told me I wasn't really serious was essentially defining what I was doing, perhaps for their own sake as much as mine. Many other patterns in the letters fall under this general category of being other-oriented. Forty or more people used the phrase "I (or we) care" at some point in their correspondence -- a simple enough thing to say, but for the most part the pages and pages that some people wrote could have been distilled to those two words. It would be interesting to re-check these 40+ people to see how many of them who stated their concern so plainly left some means of contacting them, since an anonymous "I care" is almost worthless in terms of possible tangible results. I do remember, however, that quite certainly a few of these people did remain anonymous, apparently believing that simply showing their concern was enough reason for anyone to stay alive. I'm not sure if such letters were written more to assuage the writers' consciences than to answer another's cry for help, and I'm not eager to say that such letters are more negative in emotional affect than others -- but such thoughts would bear study. As a footnote, it is interesting to see that many of the "carers" took it for granted that I would receive quite a bit of mail, like this Harvard graduate student: "Finally it might be pointed out that a world in which people try to respond to your question because of a concern for you might indeed be a world in which life could well be worth living" (#98).

Related to this group is an even larger group of people who stated in their letters that it was necessary (and vital) to either "know" me or talk to me in order to help solve my problem. Here I am sure that only a small minority did not leave either a full address or phone for further contact. Typical of this type of response is this quote from a letter from a Methuen man who gave his address: "Of course, your course of sorrow could be anything -- I don't know and am therefore limited in giving advice . . . If you need a friend, feel free to write to me" (#115). Perhaps the wording of the ad created a built-in response like this, since so little is told about me that any well-meaning and half-way intelligent person wanting to help would have to say I must know more about you before I can help you. After all, is not this a tactic used again and again by the suicide prevention worker? It is debatable, of course, how many writers who said they had to know me better intended that as a strategy to keep me from popping the pills. I divided this category into two sub-headings, one called "must know you" and the other "must talk to you"; as could be expected, the number in the former was eight times larger than the number in the latter (and it must be remembered these statistics are only sketchy in character). It is easier to say, "it's almost too obvious that we . . . don't know you even slightly and can't actually say something relevant or valid. Maybe by chance I can touch on something . . . but better than this is an effort . . . to relate to a person. Here it's more the relating to a paper than you" (#136) and then leave the letter unsigned and completely untraceable, than it is to say "I hope you'll write back to me and tell me about your problems and more about yourself so that maybe I can help you" (#139) and leave an address. Yet even though it is obvious that the more concerned belong with the latter, I can't shake the feeling that to many writers, the whole thing was an exciting escapade, a mystery to be solved. This is especially the case among the ten or so letters in which people hypothesized out loud the reasons I might have for killing myself and followed them by simple replies. Of course, the entire sample could be rated in terms such as these, i.e., how much mystery intrigued the writer to respond; the letters run the gamut from containing something as impersonal as a pamphlet with no personal remarks at all (#47) to something as totally opposite as a picture of a cute girl, complete with her measurements and address (#26).

Branching from the specific one-other-oriented

letter is a separate but related category of those people who suggest I either help others or look at others less fortunate than myself in order to divert my mind from my own troubles. There is also a similarly small group of people who tell me to think of my parents, friends or teachers before committing suicide in another effort to direct my attention away from my self. All of these categories (25 letters in all) follow Shneidman's suggestion that the prevention worker attempt to widen the caller's perspective or to change his routine, But before I discuss this facet of the letters, there is a small but odd group of at least seven people who use Others in a very specialized manner; the only way I could code it was by the one word "We." This phenomenon is vaguely apparent in this Boston man's letter: "I for one will feel let down if you are not (there to see the sun come out again), because we need more help fighting" (#2). And the pattern reaches a climax in a student's letter written in hip terminology and laden down with paranoid complexes, e.g. ". . .if all us poor bastards give up, we leave the shitty place to those obscene Feds and all the other pricks who make the world shitty. . . . Because you know what will happen when we've gone -- the Feds take over" (#118). This is more than merely saying "I know where you're at, I've been there," it is forming a clique of the select few potential suicides who apparently by virtue of their desperation are qualified to become beatified. The letters which follow this pattern are similar to acceptance forms from clubs, as if the statement that I realize the world is "shitty" has qualified me to join the elite aware bunch.

This leads me to a footnote of sorts in order to report that quite a few of the responses take it for granted that because I can visualize the possibility of my suicide, I must be extraordinarily sensitive and an interesting person to know. The paranoid student quoted above ends his letter by saying, "I wish you would write to me, if you feel like writing. Some of the people I admire tremendously have attempted suicide, I guess they are such complex and interesting persons I find a lot in them to like." This seems to be an incredibly unwarranted assumption, until one realizes that the publicized suicides are almost always those of talented people who have created in spite of suffering but eventually succumbed to The Evil World. Nevertheless, one of the three people who told me that he or she had attempted suicide was admittedly an everyday housewife with no pretense to being extra-sensitive. What I think these particular responses show is the opposite of the "elitist" variety; here, the writer is attempting to find someone better than himself, someone he can look up to. The fact that both patterns are found in the same letter (#118 for one) does not counteract the hypothesis.

Up to this point, I have not discussed the more active reasons which people submitted for my perusal; calling up someone on the telephone is essentially a passive act. Many letters contained lists of suggested activities along with the usual natural phenomena (sunsets, rain, etc.) Quite a large segment (approx. 26) quoted another source, usually a poem that had something specifically or tangentially related to suicide and/or death. No one person was quoted more than once except for Rod McKuen (3 times, each a different poem), e.e. cummings (twice) and Dylan Thomas (twice, both "Do not go gentle..."). But I would class all quotations as well as references to whole books (e.g., The Tibetan Book of the Dead (#140) or The Floating Opera, the latter mentioned at least three times) as suggestions of a passive nature -- although certainly if I had been serious, the act of going to a bookstore to purchase John Barth's novel would have been a highly un-passive action in relation to the passivity of depression and death.

Twenty-five or more people suggested that I change my daily routine, and many gave concrete ideas for how to go about doing so. Here again the tactics follow the directions put forward by Shneidman; some letters actually included the phrase, "widen your perspective." The basic statement usually alluded to doing something out of the ordinary, such as this suggestion from an Amherst girl: "O.K., wait for a sunny day, get up in the morning thinking 'This is the very first day of the rest of my life.' And forget all the pressures on you and just go out and do things you wouldn't usually do. Crazy, fun things that you'd usually never even consider" (#135). Less frivolous types of suggestions follow in the scale, like ". . .have you tried all possible alternatives toward a change in your style of life?" (#37), and finally people got much less general and more specific, coming up with such "crazy, fun things" as ". . .the Students International Meditation Society on 27 Concord Avenue . . . Go there please and talk with someone . . . . Also go to the

Sanae Restaurant . . . It could possibly be that your state of mind is due to an imbalance in your diet." (#102).

Again, however, the above suggestions are either individual-oriented or oriented to an amorphous group of others, which leads me back to the second half of my original other-oriented discussion about those people who tell me to look at others less fortunate, then to help others less fortunate, and finally to "need someone." I'm not really sure why I find these categories more potent than the probably more creative and inventive ones previously mentioned; perhaps it's due to the trend of Shneidman's lectures, which emphasize one-to-one contact between the potential suicide and one other. Perhaps also it's due to the widely-held belief that most suicides are committed because of intolerable loneliness which can only be remedied by the concern and eventual love of another person; certainly this belief is evident in the letters when one considers that 29 mention I should need someone and 37 tell me they care.

Some responses urge me to look at others less fortunate than myself in an effort to show me that my problems are not truly that bad, implying that my ad was really allowing myself to wallow in self-pity. Says one Salem girl, "There are young people who die every day, but they have no choice" (#1). Quite a few people say I should rejoice because I have that choice to make between life and death; these letters take on an existential attitude toward suicide, sometimes quoting Sartre, while prompting me to take my despair as a starting, rather than an ending, point. An interesting sideline here is the comparison of two extreme views of despair: "The greatest thing in the World is being in the position you are in now and -- what next, huh? -- and overcoming it" (#2) vs "DESPAIR IS THE ABSOLUTE EXTREME of self-love" (#131) The next step, however, from looking around at others is to help those others, e.g., "One reason for living is that maybe you can help someone else" (#3). Perhaps the most explicit statement of this attitude can be found in the letter from the Brazilian minister, who drew a chart of the small amount of his countrymen who advance past the second grade and said, "The reasons for living are the needs in the world about us, and people to fill those needs. . . .There is a tremendous need in the world for helping people to have just those abilities that you already have . . . . No one can deny that the world needs to be better than it is, and you can have a part in making it better. YOU ARE NEEDED!" (#112).

It is highly indicative of the whole sample that in only one paragraph of that letter just quoted the word "need" is used five times. So many people implore me to need someone, so that my initial reaction of surprised humor to the command had to be modified to deeper thought. How is it possible to tell a person to need another? It is conceivable that a few of the large number thought that the M 21 studt had never thought it possible to need someone, yet the majority of those who theorized my reasons included the possibility of love lost or love not found. Probably because of my own experiences, the simple suggestion that I pick up a girl is ludicrous -- what if this non-existent person had had bad experience on top of worse experience with the opposite sex, or if he found it difficult to meet anyone on the most casual basis, or if he were homosexual? Saying something like, "You've just got to wait to find one to help you put meaning back into your life" (#18) is to me an acceptable position, as is saying "Get out into the working world, communicate with people who are not all wrapped up in intellectual destructive games" (#73); but to naively end a letter with "Love others and They will love <u>you</u>" (#78) is to me pointless and essentially negative, although certainly not meant in that manner by the writer. I can only equate such statements with the inane prevention worker who told her caller to see a psychiatrist. Yet so many people use that tactic that there must be something more to it than thoughtlessness (if majority rule applies in this sort of situation).

A similarly offensive pattern found in at least 20 letters was the tendency to call me a coward and to urge me to fight. I don't consider the latter particularly annoying, since it does offer an active suggestion which was usually followed by the more concrete idea of changing my routine. But browbeating has never been especially attractive to me, and it appears even less so in the context of what the letters were purportedly trying to do. It is one thing to say, "No sympathy here, man. Just compassion, perhaps empathy . . ." (#7) but quite another to scream, "If you don't hold some firm beliefs or have some high-reaching goals to attain in life, then life really <u>isn't</u> worth living, so take your damn pills!" (#48) no matter how light-heartedly it is supposedly put. But my own opinions about the letters have very little to do with the study; I should merely give an example of the norm in this case and let it go at that. Okay: "Just think if things are bad now why give the world the pleasure of scratching you off as a conquest." (#83) Nevertheless, it is interesting and important to notice that the ambivalence prevalent in almost all other categories of response can be found even here -- at least two people urged me to <u>be</u> a coward and live!!

"What makes you think things will work out better when you are out of this world" (#97) and "Suicide is irrevocable" (#100) are two examples of the final major thread which ran through the sample, with once more at least twenty letters warning me that death is final and that I'll die anyway sooner or later. This falls in with the prevention worker's instructions to remind the caller that suicide is the supreme negation and that even if your death does effect change in people's attitudes toward you, you will not be around to see it. However, I fail to see this sort of reasoning being thrown at what I tried to make a very rational statement of intent. It would be necessary for the reader to project his own fantasies on my ad in order to decide that I hadn't realized that death was final -- and here again, an interesting study could involve psyching out the responses in terms of what they projected on me, although to what end I'm not certain.

The other categories I created for the study proved to have too few numbers to earn any separate discussion. Four people mentioned grass or alcohol as a good reason to stay alive (one of these four's "letter" consisted of two marijuana joints, which I'm afraid to say I haven't smoked for fear of what they may actually contain); an uncertain number listed man-made accomplishments as good reasons, e.g., music, laughter, smiles, movies, etc.; about thirteen gave the name of a person or institute I could contact, while an equal number simply told me I should talk to someone of importance; eleven or more seemed to think that joking would make me feel more at ease, while about nine reaffirmed my uniqueness as a person, and therefore my importance as an individual; and one person sent a box which included a Linus plastic doll, a key, a map of North America, magazine clippings reading "Introducing Kindness" and "call"-- and a peach pit.

The pornography of death is a subject that has not eluded even this study, even though it is relegated to a very small segment. But a measurable number of people followed the lead of this Mt. Holyoke student when she said, "I want you to know that I don't often go in for this kind of thing" (#154) as if writing to a potential suicide were something risque and faintly obscene. It is easy to imagine such answers to a request for a female flugel-horn player or any of the other usual personal ads in B.A.D. but it is rather inappropriate for a letter in answer to a cry for help. Such responses might be classified under the self-congratulatory type, since proclaiming that you're doing the unusual implies you should be patted on the back; but one can't rule out the licentious quality such statements entail, and I believe this to be one of the more significant findings of the survey.

The time has come to wrap up and finish with violin crescendos and happy tears. But it is truly difficult to make fun of the large number of people who cared enough to send their very best, from the person who sent in an advanced calculus equation and an admonition (#120), to the person who wrote on a shining page with a color photo of apple blossoms and a printed message reading We're Celebrating Apple Blossom Time, "I already did it!! it's a drag -- screw it -- go fishing -- buy a park bench" (#39). Indeed, one of the most difficult decisions concerning the study was how to answer these people, so many of whom asked me to tell them my decision either verbally, in writing, or through another ad in B.A.D. At first I thought I'd asked the paper if they'd consider printing a small article about the experiment as something to lift up people's spirits in the spring; but after much thought and consultation, my final solution was to put another ad in the personals section which read "Tis spring and I'm still alive, thanks to all of you. Box D-673." It may be too impersonal, but it doesn't break anyone's illusions and accomplishes the purpose of soothing their anxieties. So many writers were so upset by my plea that at one point in their letters they broke down and simply pleaded back "Don't" or "You just can't" --and I think a response as simple as "I didn't" is more than adequate to give them back their sense of goodness and life in this no-so-gentle spring.

Chapter 6

The Funeral Industry in Boston

Jonathan Baird

Mr. A. E. Long of the Long Funeral Home ("Service is a Long word") leaned back from his desk, placed his hands together, looked briefly at the full color 8x10 photograph of his wife and children and said with great sincerity, "Our function is to provide counseling to families in need at a very important time, to relieve them of the burden of worrying about the arrangements for the funeral service."

Mr. Long's grandfather founded the establishment in 1876, then more a workshop than the elaborate building that now houses "the oldest funeral home in Cambridge." Today the Long enterprise has under its roof several viewing chambers (or "slumber rooms"), casket display rooms, a basement area the secrets of which remain unseen to the non-professional, two funeral chapels, and a staff of eight including two secretaries. Mr. Long's picture gazes understandingly from a large ad in the Harvard Square subway station while the yellow pages sing the praises of its air-conditioning, pipe organ, and "reception facilities."

The growth of the funeral industry in Boston and the rest of the United States has been enormous. When the first A. E. Long founded his establishment, his functions were very limited; Jessica Mitford says in her American Way of Death (1963, p.199):

> The undertakers job was primarily custodial. It included supplying the coffin from a catalogue or from his establishment, arranging the folding chairs, taking charge of the pall-bearers, supervising the removal of the coffin and loading it into the hearse, and in general doing the necessary chores until the body was lowered into the grave.

Services and care for the dead were done largely

by the family and funerals were simple, small, unceremonius. Cemeteries were usually churchyard ones: "floral tributes" were, if not discouraged, certainly minimal. The entire service was very personal and the importance of the body very small.

While the funeral industry has grown in pretentiousness and plasticity, the conservatism and addiction to tradition that is the soul of Boston has protected her from the disease that has spread so rapidly in the funeral trade throughout America. The virtues of colonial life are here along with the vices and in funeral practices these virtues are clearly shown. The presence of the universities in and around Boston has also slowed down the process of "modernization" in funeral practices. Not as wound up in status symbols and less exposed to the mass media (or large amounts of money) the people related to the universities don't get sucked into the game of the "bier barons." This is not to suggest that the American Way of Death hasn't infected Boston, for it certainly has, but the funeral director has been forced to work with this tradition instead of throwing it out as he would obviously prefer to do.

Mr. Chester H. Eastman of Eastman Funeral Service Inc., when asked about caskets, emphatically affirmed an inquiry on whether simple wood caskets were used. In the funeral trade, a great deal of profit is made in the casket sale. Scientific methods have been developed in the trade magazines for arrangements in casket display rooms; the art of quoting prices as "$120 more" or "$60 less" rather than $727 has been finely developed. Descriptions of caskets border on the ridiculous, such as the one Jessica Mitford (p.57) notes of the "Valley Forge" model: ". . .designed to reflect the rugged, strong, soldier-like qualities associated with Valley Forge. . .symbolizes the solid, dependable, courageous American ideals so bravely tested at Valley Forge. . ." Inside are such innovations as "Beautyrama Adjustable Soft- Foam Bed" and "600 Aqua Supreme Cheney Velvet, magnificently quilted and shired." The manufactured cost of these caskets is a small fraction of the selling price and nowhere can the key aspects of the funeral trade be seen clearer than the fantastically equipped casket. Faced with a fact of funeral directing life, the directors are quick to adjust and cater to it. When occasional criticism of the funeral industry touches them they point out the reasonableness of their business and claim they in no way intend to alter their present service.

But as one moves outside Boston, one can see what the trade will do if given some rope. As near as Arlington, funeral practices become more extravagant and in places like Wellesley and Milton, the colonial spirit is obscenely burlesqued in Georgian buildings with columns and architraves. The suburbs are clearly the lucrative market in the Boston area and all the aspects of the modern American funeral industry are present.

The largest Boston House is J. S. Waterman & Sons; they handle all religions and ethnic groups. But many establishments deal with a particular group. A. E. Long & Son is the largest Protestant house in Cambridge; Daniel O'Brien takes mostly Catholics and has the highest trade volume in Cambridge. Levine Chapels is the most popular Jewish undertaker, followed by Benjamin Solomon. Berlund in Arlington takes on the Swedish residents and so on. Houses appeal particularly to their age, a factor that appeals to tradition-conscious Bostonians. A. E. Long can remember no new mortuary since he's taken over. He cites the enormous capital needed to start a business, over $200,000 with no guarantee of immediate return. People come to a house because friends or relatives were handled there and a new enterprise can't hope to attract many customers for a very long time. If someone wishes to go into business, he generally buys an existing home and retains the name for at least five years. The houses that don't change hands like this, a majority, are like inheritances, remaining in the family.

The nature of the funeral transaction is partly responsible for the expansion of the death industry. The person who is arranging for a burial generally is perturbed, and many emotions run through his, or more usually, her mind. Guilt may sometimes be present, guilt in the form of the question, "Maybe I could have done something," guilt perhaps at being alive while another is dead. Desire to make up for this guilt, or simply an honest desire to show one's love for someone when he or she was alive results in a determination to give the deceased the best funeral possible. This plays right into the funeral director's hands, since the trade is always prepared to offer some new "extra" to further show love for the dead. Thus, the familiar refrain of every funeral director, "We're only giving the public what it wants." Mr. Long reitereated this several times with a touch of weary annoyance at a "frequent misconception." But in such a situation the suggestion of a person obviously experienced in "how these things are done" has enormous weight. The director, with a practiced sincerity guides the family through a casket display room which shows only the most expensive models. If urged he will move to a less expensive showroom, all the while reminding his client of the importance of showing his or her devotion. The family has had little contact with funeral arrangements, with the pros and cons of embalming, burial against cremation, viewing the body, etc. With a little bit of twisted logic many of the mortician's arguments are compelling. Added to this is the frequent concern for "keeping up with the Jones'" and obtaining a funeral that is "worthy of a person's station in life."

These elements all drive up the cost and scale of a funeral. When Jessica Mitford wrote <u>American Way of Death</u> in 1963, the price of a funeral for an average adult was $1,405. There has been little change although the person who is positive of what he wants and is not about to get carried away can generally now get away with about $300 for the whole thing, less than in the early '60's. Boston is below the national average, although how much none of the directors will say. No one will give any figures on his trade volume or average cost of each transaction but those asked agreed that it costs less to die in this city.

In America especially, we relegate the idea of death to the back of our minds; our society is concerned with youth and life, an attitude that manifests itself in many ways that need not be treated here. But the effect of this taboo is that as we sweep the thought of death under the carpet we also repress all the aspects of it too. When I mentioned my interviewing activities to several friends, they winced and said, "I don't want to talk about it. . ." Thus, many people simply don't take a good look at the abuses of the funeral industry. Disposal of the dead for most people is such an unpleasant task that the sooner it is over with the better. People who have been badly burned by the funeral trade don't want to dwell on their experience. They say that it won't happen to them again and often consider criticism of the funeral to be disrespectful to their dead relative.

As always when a subject is taboo, several myths pop up that no one will force himself to think about long enough to explode them. Many of these concern embalming. Directors used to claim that embalming prevented decomposition. The dead person would eternally remain as his survivors last saw him through modern techniques. A slogan of the industry was "everlasting security for your Loved One." In the late forties, the case of August Chelini v. Silvio Nieri, a funeral director, in a California court completely exploded this myth. Chelini was one of the few people who did want all the aspects of the American funeral for his dead mother, especially the "everlasting security." He was happily obliged by Nieri who assured him that embalming and a sealed metal casket would provide this. Chelini, after the funeral, began to suspect that the crypt his mother lay in might be invaded by the great amount of insects he saw at the cemetery. After a year or so, the 57-year old mechanic and garage owner became so concerned that he had his mother disintered, only to find, as the doctor with him said, that "this is a hell of a mess and a hell of a poor job of embalming in my opinion." Chelini then sued for $50,000. In the resulting trial it was learned that the practice of embalming can in no way slow down decomposition of a body, and the metal "seal-type" casket only hastens the natural process. Chelini was awarded $10,900 while the funeral trade squirmed uncomfortably. Embalming is also cited as a public health service, especially in the case of communicable diseases. Jessica Mitford did some extensive research on this subject and finds no evidence outside the funeral trade to support this contention.

Both Mr. Long and Mr. Eastman contend that viewing the body in a "slumber room" or open casket is effective grief therapy. In Evelyn Waugh's satiric novel The Loved One (1948) a "mortuary hostess" gives Dennis Barlow the rationale for this practice (p.62):

> The leave taking is a very great source of consolation. Often the Waiting Ones (survivors) last saw their Loved Ones on a bed of pain surrounded by all the gruesome concomitants of the sick room or the hospital. Here they see them as they knew them in Buoyant Life, transfigured with peace and happiness. At the funeral they have time for a brief look only as they file past. Here in the Slumber Room they can stand as they like, photographing a last beautiful memory on the mind.

To create this "Beautiful Memory Picture" (the trade's term) an enormous amount of energy is expended. The recreation of a corpse is looked on by most in the trade as an art form in itself. Waugh describes such an artist inspired by the cosmetician he is preparing his subject for (p.117):

> And behold, where once had been a grim line of endurance there was now a smile! It was masterly. It needed no other touch. Mr. Joyboy stood back from his work removed his gloves and said: "For Miss Thanatgenos."

Despite the trade's justification, one finds evidence supporting it to be highly elusive. My own reaction to the painted restoration of my grandmother was that I thought it obscene and this sentiment is mirrored by all I have spoken to. Jessica Mitford obtained similar reactions and despite impressive research found no psychiatric opinion that viewing the corpse contributed in any way to grief therapy. The North American continent is apparently the only place in the world that such a practice is tolerated. The attitude of the foreigner to the idea is expressed beautifully in a letter to Mitford from an English friend (p.76):

> It shook me rigid to get there and find the casket open and poor old Oscar lying there in his brown tweed suit wearing suntan makeup and just the wrong shade of lipstick. If I had not been extremely fond of the old boy I have a horrible feeling I would've giggled. Then and there I decided I could never face another American funeral - even dead.

If heaven exists somewhere, many Boston residents think it may be somewhere in the Mt. Auburn St. Cemetery. Lying just outside Cambridge on Rt. 2, the cemetery, while not the largest in Boston, is certainly the most impressive. Gentle hillsides, valleys, foliage, churches, streams, and ponds all beautifully laid out stretch as far as the eye can see, which is not a great distance since the terrain varies so much one gets a strange feeling of privacy, surrounded by this pastoral landscape. Paths and roads criss-cross throughout with such names as "Moss Rd.", "Ivy Lane," and "Primrose Path." The variety of the foliage is incredible and each carefully pruned tree is labelled with its generic family. In the spring it is especially lovely, as all colors of blossoms are evident. There are millions of flowers, some planted on gravesites and the air is heavy with the scent. Monuments are tastefully arranged, varying in scale from simple slabs to a huge reproduction of the sphinx with a portrait face. A slightly altered version of John Harvard marks one grave. Many of the monuments have very early dates on them; there is an obviously new marker with "1640" on it, showing that many redesign the gravesites of their ancestors. Epitaphs range from the last names to such dripping sentimentalities as "We shall meet in heaven to part no more." Some grave lots say "Father-Mother" and list the first names of their children who died later and were laid under smaller stones next to their parents. Others read "Husband-Wife." Family plots have an address written on the stairs, but all the gravesites have numbers such as "2245 Oak Lane." The office building is in red brick, early English Gothic, perhaps copied from the palace at Hampton Court outside London. Huge gates which mark the entrance display the message, "Then shall the dust return to the earth as it was and the spirit shall return to God who gave it." The place is simply incredible and no one who spends any time in Cambridge should miss it.

Out on the west coast and in many other areas too, the super-cemetery has emerged, the leading one being Forest Lawn in Los Angeles, the model for Evelyn Waugh's "Whispering Glades." All that is at Mr. Auburn is there tenfold, plus many other features such as independent statuary, several "romantic" spots for the enormous number of people who visit even with no relative buried there, and an entire mortuary establishment, making it a "one stop" enterprise, a supermarket for the dead. In Boston, difficulties in obtaining large amounts of land as well as local tradition has held back similar projects. There are smaller burial grounds here and the cemeteries have not become quite as plastic. There are even a few simple areas in Boston, a vision that is fast becoming obsolete.

Cemetery land is tax-free, an old tradition in this country formulated in several Supreme Court decisions. The business it appears at first glance, is non-profit, and its income also tax-free. But the operation is hardly so since the promoters, sometimes a land-holding company, work out an arrangement whereby the cemetery will get only, say, 50 per cent of the income while the promoters get the other half. The cemetery is still non-profit but the men behind it are raking in awesome amounts (also tax-free). Investment in cemeteries is much more profitable than in regular land because it can be intricately subdivided and charges can be levied for maintenance as well as monuments. Across the street from the cemetery office is a concern that makes gravestones. One doesn't go in and ask outright if the same people are running both cemetery and monument business; the company names are different. But it might not be an unreasonable surmise that the two lead back to the same promoters.

As cemeteries become crowded, a new invention has broken the space barrier: the community mausoleum. Piling crypts on top of each other and charging an average of $720 plus "maintenance costs" for each one, the cemetery promoters have hit on a most lucrative idea, with unlimited opportunities. The "tenement mausoleums" haven't really caught on in Boston, however, despite their staggering expansion throughout the rest of the country.

A recent phenomenon in the funeral industry is "pre-need" buying. The practice was originated by the cemeteries; negotiation was carried on through the funeral director, who was not about to urge spending great amounts of money on a gravesite since it might result in less "investment" in his own services. So the cemeteries created a way to get around the director: "pre-need" door to door selling. This has enabled the cemeteries to obtain the capital to build before anyone is actually buried: the operation is thus self-financing.

The salesman, who is called a "memorial counselor," uses inflation as his first argument. His second is that of protecting the survivor (generally the wife in the sales pitch) from overspending at a time of emotional strain. Customers buy because of "the aura of genteel respectability conferred by ownership of cemetery property" and the self-congratulations for "planning ahead." But they ignore the publicly owned cemeteries where gravesites are much cheaper, fail to see that the practice of "pre-need" sales has pushed up the price of a cemetery plot, and might be cremated for all they really cared.

The funeral directors then picked up the practice.

Mr. Long said there was "a good deal" of pre-need buying not only for the cemeteries but for his own establishment as well. "These are mostly aging people who have lived alone for some time," he elaborated. Neither he nor Mr. Eastman volunteered percentages. The latter expressed his pleasure with the idea, felt that the industry was offering security and assurance of "adequate care" for those who bought. More elaborate justifications are noted by Evelyn Waugh who has the "mortuary hostess" speak of bringing the fear of death into the open and removing such anxiety by preparation now. Her spiel involves a strange interweaving of the fear of dying and the fear of creating economic burdens at death, spiced with general truisms, "scientific data" and quotes from Hamlet.

Faced with the growth of the American Way of Death, many people are forming "memorial societies." The purpose of these is stated in the pamphlet "Memorial Associations; what they are and how they are organized" put out by the Cooperative League of the U.S.A. (Nora,1962):

> Memorial Associations and their members seek modesty, simplicity and dignity in the funeral arrangements over which they have control. This concern for the spiritual over material values has revealed that a "decent burial" or other arrangement need not be elaborate.

A trade magazine, The National Funeral Service Journal, as quoted by Jessica Mitford, said (p.267): "The movement appeals most strongly to the visionary, ivory tower eggheads of the academic fraternity", a description that fits Boston and Cambridge in particular quite nicely. The societies are especially popular in Boston. The largest is the Memorial Society of Massachusetts at 874 Beacon St., but there are others in the surrounding communities. The members contribute moderate amounts of money and work through a funeral director who agrees to handle all the society's business. Finding such a director is difficult but not impossible; the extra business, even at lower prices, is enormously pleasant to a house that is not at the top of the trade. The Long Home is not one of these. Mr. Long shook his head, wearily perplexed; "I don't know. . .they accept all this money and I don't know what they do with it. They could get the same service here for the same price." When asked if he did any of their work, he replied, "There's no sense in going along with them - no, we don't cooperate."

The funeral trade has been exposed to a great deal of criticism in the last decade and has grown more and more sensitive. All the Boston houses contacted greeted the request for an interview with suspicion and only two were accepted with reluctance. The remaining three didn't openly refuse interviews but rather said their business volume was unmanageable that day but to try again tomorrow. This went on for four days at O'Brien's near Central Square when a Miss Hanlon who apparently runs that branch, talked briefly over the phone about the poor publicity and no chance to respond. Despite frequent assurances that the research was being conducted with an open mind and that this would be the best way for the trade to defend itself, she would not even grant a ten-minute interview. The other houses were not as frank but equally adept at putting off the request, Waterman's for three days and Levine for two.

One of the most difficult things to get a hold of are the trade magazines. They are found in no library in the Boston area. I asked Mr. Long for one or two and he sent me to Miss Hanlon at O'Brien's. She told me Mr. Long had them too, but wouldn't give them up and she wouldn't either. She compared it to "going into a chemical factory and asking to see the formulas." and said I would learn nothing more than technical data such as new embalming fluids. Even though it was pointed out that magazines were of a different nature than chemical formulas of one particular plant, she remained obdurate and wouldn't surrender the journals.

The industry has reacted viciously to criticism from more widely read discussions than this one. Two well known ones were Davidson's "High Cost of Dying" in Collier's in 1951 and Tunley's "Can You Afford to Die?" in the Saturday Evening Post in 1961. The trade was shaken and its press responded with charges of atheism and communist sympathies. The second article was particularly resented, for it offered concrete suggestions for remedy: the memorial societies previously mentioned. The most famous investigation has, of course, been Jessica Mitford's American Way of Death. Even six years after the book appeared, the directors are still shaking. A. E. Long, when asked about the book, quickly became upset: "Money. . .that's all she was out for. If people want to pay good money for a thing like that . . .carry it around with them. . . I don't care." He warmed up and became really talkative for the first time in 45 minutes. Admittedly there are a few bad establishments - there are in any profession. There are corrupt lawyers. . .you know a few corrupt lawyers, don't you?" I replied I imagined there were, quite embarrassed at being the cause of this outburst. He continued, "Sure there are, but compared to the huge numbers of good establishments, the corrupt ones are an infinitesimal amount."

Despite Mr. Long's protestations, it seems there is a good deal more to be said about the evils of the funeral trade than he cares to include. While Boston has been spared some of what has happened throughout America, it is still very much infected by the modern death industry.

References

Mitford, Jessica. The American Way of Death. New York: Simon and Schuster, 1963.

Nora, Fred. Memorial Associations. New York: Cooperative League of the U.S.A., 1962.

Waugh, Evelyn. The Loved One. New York: Dell, 1948.

PART III

SOME SEQUELAE OF DEATH

Chapter 7

Wake

Daniel B. Gordon

What do you do when you can't make or let or wish any more tears flow? You go to a funeral wake.

The apartment was handsome and even imposing when it was empty. There was a foyer paved with marble and walled with mirrors, leading into a large, uncarpeted living room, a small and stuffy "study", or through a white and starched passageway paved in blue carpet to dining and bedrooms. But it was filled now, and through the front door was filling more with people--couples, families, old dowagers, young men--who milled through the rooms, making the apartment maybe less handsome, but no less imposing.

All of these people, I thought, bear some relationship to Peter. Coming here is their claim. It's really a party, a get-together. I was sitting with a drink and a well-composed face near the doorway of the study, oddly proud that I bore not just some relationship to Peter, but was his brother.

Was? I had slipped stupified into the use of the past tense toward Peter, but now I was amazed by the ease with which it came to mind and to lip, as if I had always been ready for Peter to hang himself late at night. I pictured that to myself, trying to press it hard into the grey cells of my brain, him hanging, feet dangling, in a college room no longer his castle but his tomb. I tried to stir my sorrow by thinking of this over and over, but I was too tired and too bitter at the party spirit of the other guests to affront them in this way, for I visualized my crying as an affront to them in the height of their grim gaiety. So it was only I who was affronted by my grief, and only I who clenched his teeth and was gay.

"Stan?" I looked up. My eyes had been closed and staring downwards to the earth. It was Mrs. Cohen, standing steadily in front of me, her eyes searching my eyes. God knows what she wanted to find there.

"Hello," I said, rising and smiling warmly. She was the mother of a girlfriend of mine, a girl who had twice slept with Peter long ago. She stuck out her arms and embraced me, and I held her lightly with my one free hand, wishing it to rove over her back and down to her soft ass.

"How are you?" she said when I moved away.

"Fine," I said, still smiling. "Well, all right. I mean, I'm in pretty good shape."

"Good," she said seriously. "Cathy wanted to come down badly"--then why didn't she, I thought--" and she told me to have you see her when you get back."

"Okay," I said, "I got the message and will see Cathy, besides which I want to." She smiled ironically. I don't know how else I could have said it.

"Are you drunk, Stan?" she asked, smiling again. "Your mother wouldn't approve." She was an old friend of my mother's.

"I think she would today," I replied, thinking of how my father had forced me to drink some Scotch the night before, "So that you can get some damn sleep at least tonight," he said.

"No," she said hastily, "You have a right to drink tonight. But be kind to your parents, Stan. They really need that."

"Sure," I said soothingly, as if it were she who needed the comfort. My passion seemed to have risen through the sodden feeling of the booze. I imaged Cathy before me, her nipples touching almost the middle of my chest as she stood there, breathing more slowly and staring, like her mother, into my eyes. I looked at Mrs. Cohen; her nipples would touch mine; I looked away, down darkly at her feet, then up the sheathed legs and her dress-I looked back at her eyes.

"But who will be a comfort to me?" I asked her.

"I think you can take care of yourself. Or you

can ask for what you need."

Peter couldn't do that very well, I thought. What makes you think I can any better? And you, turning in my head to the body of Peter as I had seen it this afternoon, what the hell are you trying to do?

"Yeah," I said, smiling sagely to Mrs. Cohen. "Excuse me, I'd like to get another drink," I said, pointing to the half-full glass. She stood aside and let me walk into the hall.

"But she said that instead. . ."

"I didn't really want to press it. . ."

". . .in three or four days, I guess. . ."

"They don't want that, though. . ."

"Have you seen him? Where did. . ."

"Oh yes, I was at home when they called. . ."

I walked by and through ten different conversations, all irrelevant to any of us or what we were thinking. I wished in some way that we were all talking about Peter, shouting or screaming or swearing, and I was thankful in another that we said nothing about it at all. And perhaps they all agreed with me, because my father stopped me, and only asked if I could get him another drink. He was talking with an old man and a woman, and a young boy who was staring at him fixedly.

"Having a good time?" he asked. I shrugged.

At the bar stood Eduardo, my brother's roommate, the last person to see him alive and the first to see him dead. "Him" dead? It was not him, it was "his body", his corpse, a mouldering business of carbon and nitrogen divorced from form now forever. Eduardo was concentrating on the preparation and constitution of his drink, his back turned to all the rest of us. I had last seen him at the funeral, staring too long and too intrusively as he cried silently, until I began to cry but rather sharing the picture that he must carry around forever in his brain.

"Hey, Eduardo," I said softly.

"Stan," he said happily, smiling as if lifting the corners of his mouth cost him much sorrow and rage.

"This is really like a big party," I said, pointing back to the crowd from which we were isolated by a small open space. "Some of these people haven't seen each other for years, and for them it's just a chance for a get-together."

"Yes. The old women are gabbing together as this was their last chance." Both our faces clouded.

"Of course," I said at last. "Are you going back to Boston tonight?"

"No, I will stay with Jonathan tonight, and go back probably tomorrow morning."

"Hallowell. Have you seen him?"

"Not since the funeral ceremony. Who was that girl with him?" She had held his face in her hands as he cried.

"Her name is Pamela. She's his chick."

"Are any of them here?" Anybody young? Anybody young besides broken Eduardo.

"I haven't seen them. They said they would come."

"Ah," I said. "Well, I have to take this drink back to my father. I'll be back."

"Sure," he said, "I'll see you later."

I walked away, turning back once to catch his face unguarded by a smile, twisted into torture so acute that I wished I had not looked. He might have saved Peter's life, and had not, could not have. I wondered if I would absolve him of that guilt, if I could.

"How was Eduardo?" he asked as I handed him his drink. His tone was snappy and bored, as if he could muster very little concern for Eduardo or compassion for him but felt compelled to.

"He's as well as could be expected," I snapped back.

"That poor, stupid kid," my father said, shaking his head. "If he just--" could have called you, I thought, and told you your son was about to die, was trying to die. But then what?

"Yes," I interrupted, "if only. But he couldn't do anything, or anyhow he didn't, so what good does it do to brood about it?"

"You're right," my father said. But he admitted it without any sense of the weight that it must have cost him. "What did you think?"

"Of the funeral?" I wished before I said my next words that I had no need to say them. "Do you want to know what I think, or what Peter would have thought?"

"Both," he said, looking hurt around the edges of his eyes.

"Okay," I said, in a duller voice, "I thought it was very good, very moving. Peter would have thought it was too religious."

My father laughed. "You're right. What a sense of humor that boy had." Then his voice trailed off, "What a lot of everything he had, and now it's all gone, so stupid," and then he began to cry.

What was I to say? Don't worry? It's all right? Well, he's dead now? I mumbled, "Don't worry," as softly as I could and still be heard, and walked away from him.

At the end of the living room was a set of windows overlooking the Park. I walked to them, and peered out at the empty stretches of the snow-covered trees and fields, the lights from the streetlamps inside the park itself a maze or a jungle surrounding the streaming cars. I could not see the street directly below without opening the window and leaning over the edge, and it was both too cold to attempt it and too dangerous. Besides, I thought, someone in the room might think I was trying to jump. Those possibilities were no longer out of the question, whereas no one would have conceived of them before. Before. I wondered if I would only measure time from then on as before or after. . .it.

"Stan." I turned around and faced my uncle, one of my mother's brothers, perhaps the person I felt closest to at the wake. He was the only one, it seemed, who felt I deserved some form of sympathy, perhaps the only one who could deliver it so that it worked.

"Hi," I replied. "Do you know what the Irish say at funeral wakes? 'Sorry for your trouble.' I think that's very beautiful."

"Mrs. Cohen said you looked unhappy."

"Am I happy? Should I be happy now? Of course I'm unhappy. I just don't want to make a big thing out of it. So everyone projects their fears onto me. What did she think? That I was going to, going to kill myself, too?"

"I don't think that's what she was afraid of," he said, putting down his drink.

"Well, I'm not that stupid, or scared, or whatever it takes."

"Tell me, Stan, what are you all frightened of?"

"Young kids?" He nodded. "I don't know," I said, reluctant to discuss it, realizing that I, too, was frightened of what I might do. "I guess, sort of the fear of being rejected by another person, or being humiliated if you ask them for help. Just scared to death of that." I smiled at the joke.

"You're right," he said, smiling slightly, "It can scare someone to death. Why is that? Can you tell me? Can you tell me why you're scared of another person much like yourself, just as scared of you, and that's not such a frightening, horrifying thing; and why instead you aren't scared of dying, of all the chances you take and the dangers you risk? Why aren't people scared of cars? Why by other people?"

"I don't know," I said softly. He had spoken very urgently. "But death scares me. It scares the shit out of me."

"But why people, Stan, can you tell me that?"

"They're threatening. They have a power over you."

"I know," was all that he would say after a short silence. Then he walked over to the couch and sat down. He invited me over with a swift, beckoning look, and I came and sat on the chair next to him, lighting a cigarette and looking for an ashtray. We gawked at the furniture and the photographs perched on tables around us. Finally, I think he grew too embarrassed with the silence.

"I'll be right back," he said, getting up and taking his glass with him.

"Please do," I said as beseechingly as I could. I wanted him around to help me understand what in hell was going to happen after the party was over, when I had to go to a room by myself and try to sleep. The last night had been easy with the booze and the exhaustion weighing me down deep into the sheets and into a dreamless sleep. Tonight, again, I hoped there be no dreams, for I knew keenly that they would wrack me from sleep to which I could then never return.

Peter had linked three belts together with the buckles, linked them and strung them over the door between his living room and his bedroom. Then he had slipped the last belt into a prefabricated noose over his head, standing, I guessed, on a chair, and then he had jumped or leaped or slipped, the objects in that room, which were <u>his</u>, staring at him with whatever consciousness they possessed while he stared a last time at them, blurred by the sudden impact of all these sights seen for the last time and then, when he had thought in an instant that this was truly his last sight, hadn't he screamed deep in his mind, oh no, the last thought which filled him as the drop of his body stopped him, the last thought oh no oh no blinding him.

"Young man, do you mind if I sit down?"

"I too?"

Blinding him. I looked up at two old men who spoke in chorus, standing on either side of my chair.

"Hello," I said. "Go ahead. Please."

"Thank you," said the one who sat on the couch.

"I'm Misha," said the one who sat on the other

chair. "I do not think you remember me." He spoke with a heavily accented, grating voice.

"Oh no," I demurred politely, not remembering him, "I remember you from--"

"I'm Pasha," said the other, "And you cannot possibly remember me."

"The name is familiar," I offered.

"You are thinking of the violinist," he said.

"Heifetz?"

"No," said the one on the chair, "that's Jascha."

"Oh," I said, "No, I mean the other Heifetz."

"Of course he does," Pasha said to Misha.

"The one who plays the piano?" Misha asked.

"No, he is dead many years. When is it? When I was a young man I would hear him play."

That I could sit here, two days after my brother had killed himself, and listen to two old men discuss a mouldering pianist, impressed me strongly. My uncle returned.

"I see you're busy," he said, and gently led the two old men into conversation. I slipped away, smiling at my uncle for what did not need to be said between us.

I threaded slowly through the groups of prattling people, recognized, offered sympathy, embraced:

They had had a machine to lower my brother's coffin into the grave.

"Yes, I'll be fine, in time," I said to an aunt.

The Mourner's Kaddish is of Egyptian origin, taken by the Jews during their captivity there.

"I've been hoping to get down, but there's never been a chance," I said to her husband.

Is there, anywhere in this mess, a girl of my age whom I have known, whom I can kiss?

"When did you get in?" I said to Mrs. McElheny, after kissing her on the cheek. She was very nice, and held me nicely.

Peter was probably stoned that night, had just finished a paper on Nechaev, a Russian revolutionary.

"No, it was a very Quaker kind of ceremony," I replied to Mr. Cohen.

Or maybe he was shooting heroin. Eduardo had told my father that Peter had been taking that shit.

"Yes, it's a bad time all around."

Is he here now? Can he be, some kind of disembodied spirit, floating around the room, watching every one of us. Is he pleased?

"No, I think when you've died you are just dead, that's all," I told my younger brother firmly.

"It's Egyptian," I told an old man.

"It's too bad we can't," I said to Eduardo.

What do they all want to hear? Why talk to me? I'm innocent, all I want is a party, no corpses or embraces. I want to know what to say.

"He was stoned and he slipped. He blew it," I said to Jonathan. He didn't say anything. The night before we had walked for a long time, and he had told me that the souls of suicides were immediately reborn, because they had failed to fulfill their appropriate _karma._ Some baby stuck with Peter's soul?

The next drink was bitter and harsh, the next slow and smooth, the next contained no liquor, the next I carried but never touched. And there came a time, as I stared at the drink on the floor between my hands, when two feet stood there and called my name. I looked up and saw Marie, short and soft, her long hair growing from blond to black, her mouth resting partly open, her eyes curious and sustained. I stood as steadily as I might, and rested my hands on her shoulders, pressing them more tightly than I wished.

"Stan," she said.

"I'm very glad you're here," I said, and clasped her behind the back and she threw her arms around my shoulders. I kissed her on the lips with my eyes closed like shellfish, and then I stroked her hair back behind her ear, slowly and patiently. I had always wanted to cock her hair behind each ear, but never had I been so tender, such a clever lover, and never had she clung to me so.

"Why is it that we're so afraid of people, and so little afraid of death?" I asked her scalp.

"Did you say something, Stan?" she asked.

"Nothing. There were two old men. In the living room. They were absurd." She pressed her lips against mine, and breathed softly into my mouth.

What was it my mother had said? "He did this in rage at the people he loved, hoping their guilt would destroy them. But it's him that's destroyed, and it's us who survive." No understanding in words was possible; for my father, therefore, there was no comfort, only acceptance. For myself, I really asked for no words, because it was perfectly clear. I heard my uncle because his words made me want others again. I heard Marie because she answered, not to words, but with arms to the nameless thing that lay in my eyes, the nameless thing that is not simply grief, that is not simply loss, or hate, or fruitless hope, but is learning, is the growing knowledge that none of these things can be felt for the dead. Yet they all are, and so in Marie's arms I hoped that somewhere above us in the smoke circled the shade of my brother Peter, who had taken his life. I hoped that he watched us embrace, that he watched me begin to tear myself from him. I wanted him to gnash his teeth and drift out of all reckoning, I wanted to ruin him as he had ruined us. I wanted him to truly die if he had so chosen. I wanted so very very much to be glad.

Chapter 8

Monolithic Daddyism: An Autobiographical Account of Death

Goodwin H. Harding

Behavior is a function of experience. My experience is father, my behavior embodies him. My life, therefore, has been a tragic sacrifice to death. My experience of my father is virtual and not actual. Of course he was a real "daddy" when I was a very small child; but always, because I shall never remember the time that I did know him, he will remain a figurative person, a daily myth, Primal Father, alive, destructive, inspiring. His image is more my creation than his.

My father died when I was four. I was in the kitchen with my mother when we heard him fall, all the way down from upstairs head over heels, thump. Time stopped. A moment of putting who and what together without why. Then I stopped. Amnesia. Everything happened, nothing happened. What's the difference? Did someone scream, what do their faces say? I can only lead my memory from the empty stairs to the pale blue pajamas at this leg; it won't reach past the plaid edge of his bathrobe. One fixed scene, a photograph: his head will not be in it. Just the blood. Later my mother was talking on the phone by the grey armchair. I stood off at a distance, helpless. I'm sure the event must have terrified me absolutely, for I can still feel the numbness, and the isolation.

I remember walking in to the room with the red roses splashed all over the wallpaper; my father was reading a newspaper in bed. Why can't I think what he did or what he looked like? The roses blot him out! Horrid old ladies hiding in the patterns on the wall steal my memory, steal the image of my father. Perhaps they are a warning, a detour, a death omen to quell ambitious thoughts. Can I ever believe that I once saw his face...He was sick, I knew that. At least I could have said as much then. I wonder if it really meant anything to me. The main thing is: I knew that's where he was all the time. There was a distance between us, a hesitance. It's funny to realize that until I was eighteen, I had always thought my father died of asthma; he died of lung cancer.

One spring day the snow had almost melted, and he came outside wearing that white cap in the pictures. I am looking at him from the porch as he kneels down beside the willow tree to play with my younger sister. I have seen his face so rarely that even in memory he seems a stranger. But then, sometimes, I imagine he is kneeling down beside me, although I am still watching from above. The dreamer or the dream, the memory or the fantasy: which prompts which?

I claim only four sure memories of my father. The fourth is no more true than the first, yet it is perhaps a bit more explicit. From my point of view it is the most nostalgic, since it has become objectified in the physical world. It concerns a small rowboat which trudges back and forth across Hospital Cove harbor every summer at Cape Cod. Our family thinks of it in much the same way it would a dog, despite its rickety seats and leaky floorboards. Certainly the most child-worn boat in the harbor, its colors have changed many times. It is the only real link I have with my father. I helped him build it.

I mean I held screws, threw away scraps, and mostly got in everyone's way. I also was assigned the excruciating task of being chosen man-in-charge-of-waiting-til-it's-done, an honor of great distinction in those days. In all my years of school athletics I never knew deeper satisfaction from team spirit than the one I felt during the construction of that boat. We were a grand trio; the sense of harmony I remember has never been matched. It scares me to think seriously of what that means.

The third comrade was a friend of the family, my uncle's brother-in-law. He died when I was about seven. Until this moment I had not thought of him in over ten years. In those days I hardly noticed him, he was just another grown-up. We didn't share more activities probably because he came down to the Cape only one or two days a summer. Or I won't remember that we did. But there was always a careful, particular interest in him if I saw him lying on the deck, or sitting on the boathouse ramp, like the times you stop and wonder if what you're doing doesn't reiterate last night's dreams.

I did notice him. Maybe I wouldn't let him approach me, as if it were too painful to be reminded of the loss. When they told me he died, I listened with a special affinity.

Those are the memories of my father, the ones I consider real, all of them, just four. I have tried to demonstrate how hard it is for me to think I ever saw my father alive. Outside my mind. He has had such influence on me. People tell me of course I have, but that doesn't make much difference. How can I be sure they are memories, if not purely imagination from what I've been told. But it still doesn't matter. I would cling to them if there never was a thing Father, like a small child grappling after its mother's breast too soon snatched away. If one day, one day after years of days I happen to fix on one of these memories, long ignored, it is as though I have carried with me in the most familiar place every minute.

There are some pictures of my father in our living room, and then my mother has a few on her dresser. Their indisputable photographic reality overwhelms the attempt of my conscious mind to conjure a vivid image; consequently, it supplies an everready call to fantasy. In this sense, they are just as much a source, a cornerstone, of the myth-making process as memory.

Except for the portraits, most are shots made at the Cape. T-shirt, khaki pants, holely sneakers. Sun. Hair is lifting off my forehead, I can feel the southwest wind pick up like it does every afternoon in Buzzards Bay. High tide, my sister Wendy on his lap, and sitting there in our living room in February suddenly I'm seven years old running down the hill after rest period, wondering how fast I can put on my bathing suit and jump into that warm water.

My mother's favorite picture shows my father standing on the stern of a sailboat cutting marlin, overhead view. I think of how many pairs of sneakers I didn't want to throw away. He loved to sail, just to be out on the water Mum said. Painted, varnished, sanded, yanked boats in and out of the water, built and rebuilt them so he could belong in part to the sea. After his body was cremated, the ashes were taken out into the bay and flung to the ocean. I've always wondered who was in the boat that took him out.

I have a special fondness for the one of my father and me on the beach at low tide. I like to imagine I put that wide grin on his face, that my chubby body stuffed into all those clothes made him laugh. He is squatting down beside me so our heads are about even, watching me; our games have been interrupted. I look back puzzled towards the camera. He is no stranger in this photograph. There is a friendliness, a companionship; sort of a primitive equality that transcends size and order; a feeling of naturalness. It has been a substitute for the close relationship I had with my father in the earliest years, which my mother has told me about, but which I don't remember.

Another photograph has my father sitting on the porch step of the "big house", my grandparents summer house which overlooks the harbor. He is flanked at each knee by two cousins who were probably nine or ten years old at the time; I am jealous of their being able to sit there. Somewhere in a remote corner of my attic consciousness I can feel the desire, the need, for a father figure.

Whatever happened to him? My father. Daddy. Life. How could I forget to look for him all these years? Gone, obsolete, buried from consciousness and ego and self. I deserted him, yes, I gave up on him. But still I'm trying to trace his face through my childhood, still trying to make him alive, still trying to redeem myself. I spurned him when I should have craved him. He was a god. Lost paradise.

Yet all these same years I have kept him alive in my head, sanctified and consecrated him, begged forgiveness of him. He was lost to my conscious mind and I took him, raised him, gave birth to the dead and resurrected him, internalized him, made him me and me him, worshipped him. He was dead, so I became dead, paradise of the lost. I craved him when I should have spurned him. He was a devil. Will I give him up?

I have suffered guilt for not remembering him, not keeping him alive, and death for doing so. What kind of faith demands such sacrifice, what monolith looms over my life?

As I am sitting here now writing about myself, about my life, or my father, whichever way you want to look at it -- the everyday effect he has on my life --

it is so difficult to believe I thought of him at all until I was nineteen or twenty. Here I am not repudiating the pictures, the trinkets, the passing comments of him; nor do I disavow for a moment the knowledge that every time I sign my name I sign his, that people who knew him see him when they look at me. I am merely trying to describe the overall mood and dominating feeling: the conviction that he wasn't there. The direct experience of repression. I was my own father. I had brought myself up.

Whenever people asked me what my father did, what he thought about this or that, I would answer indifferently that he died when I was very young. It always amused me how they pretended to be so upset, so concerned, when it didn't seem to bother me at all. No, you don't have to apologize, you don't have to feel sorry, I would want to say to them, although I was really trying to convince myself. Maybe they knew what I was missing, or what I must be suffering. Maybe they were simply jealous. Anyway, he was as much a stranger in that situation as he is in memory and photographs.

Sometimes late at night while lying in bed I would remember that our family once did have a father, but he died. I tried to imagine what it would be like to have one, of my own, like other boys, how I should feel, and did I really miss one. I decided that I hadn't missed one, since I didn't ever have one, really, to miss. Or something like that. Although I could see it would have been nice at special times. On the other hand, I was constantly aware that I couldn't understand the demands and anxieties of other boys simply because I lacked the experience of a father. I knew it gave me a certain distance, or perspective, in relation to the life of my friends. Perhaps I was glad to think I had avoided particular hang-ups, not living under the immediate influence of a father. I thought I was freer to form my own opinions. There is today a great deal of truth in that.

One of the reasons why I have felt for so long that I have become my own son lies in the responsibility placed on me as the eldest son, the new "man of the family." My mother sought my opinion in many problems she had with my younger brother and sister; she trusted and respected me, and thereby made me feel equal in terms of moral authority. In this process she intuitively transmuted the character strengths of trust and self-esteem. Later, she entrusted me with further responsibility when I was invited to judge the pros and cons of my own behavior, literally take apart in the decision-making process. Although my mother punished me no more than two or three times to my knowledge, her criticism served the same function. With the enormous distinction that it was not "punishment." Even here, the framework was discussion, or argument; rarely, if ever, did she invoke a code of laws. There were complications to this system, to be sure: perhaps it stimulated a reluctance to desire more responsibility, insofar as I got too much too soon. My scales, however, show that the strengths far outweigh the weaknesses. I shall always admire my mother for this sagacity.

More important than her gift of a kind of ethical autonomy, as it relates to my general feeling during this period of being on my own, was the unfortunate process by which I began to estrange myself from my mother in order to protect myself from her implicit challenge.

I suppose the first step in this direction was taken when I learned to enjoy lying in bed at night without sleeping. I remember knocking softly on my mother's door to tell her I couldn't go to sleep. Snuggling close to her warm body was probably the original ambition behind my insomnia. Slowly she persuaded me to stay there and wait it out. I continued to lie awake, sometimes for hours, up to my freshman year in Harvard. I miss that time often, feel gypped out of what I considered to be a very important part of my life. At an early age I stopped being anxious about it, stopped being restless; I simply accepted it. Even made a habit out of it. I forgot about the old desire, it became my time, the time when I could come to know myself.

My mother usually came into my room before I turned off the lights to say goodnight. She used to kid me about puberty, pretending that she could predict when my voice was going to change by counting the scraggily hairs under my arms. Of course this made me shy and anxious before it made me smile, and I began to dread the moment when she would decide to tell me the facts of life. Awkwardly I held back from kissing her, it made me squeamish, and consequently my mother grew more insistent that I return a little affection. My will prevailed in what seemed to be at the time an embarrassing situation. As it turned out, I had already read the book she gave me, The Wonder of Life, four years earlier.

The kissing thing was soon a large symbol. The less I kissed her, the more she tried to embarrass me into doing so. If I left the house for the movies when there were people over, she would call "Come and kiss your mother before you go." She might have said it only once, but the feeling was there every time. Or coming back from a weekend visit to a friend's house, I would be expected to go over and kiss her hello. My grandmother or somebody there would say come on now you can kiss your mother. Sure I can kiss my mother but I don't want to right now, can't you see? Finally she caught on, but not before it had become a big issue. I don't like to admit that I was so tight, because I know how little it is to ask, and how much it probably hurt her. Much later she said, "Some kids just don't like to kiss their mothers, we all know that, but you're stuck with the one you've got." Damn. How could I tell her I loved her when I wouldn't kiss her, when I was afraid to put my arms around her? How could I explain that it was she who wouldn't let me kiss her when I didn't know myself? Of all things, how could I tell her that she threatened me with her love?

So I lead her to think I just wasn't the mushy type. But she was real and I was deceitful; she was living herself out while I was tying mine up in knots inside me. In the long run, at the finish where she might not be there to understand, her honesty and her love, by osmosis, will hopefully win out. For it is in this appreciation that I can gain maturity. It is the act of grace which I can bestow on the parent as the child. Forgiveness.

In a large sense, this relationship with my mother accounts for the way in which I have grown accustomed to keeping my emotions to myself. I want to unlearn that. My frigidity towards my mother during the teen years kept her apart from almost everything I was thinking about. Kindly she did not try to alter this peculiar mode of operation; she didn't try to storm the walls. I would come down to breakfast solemn, begrudging the school days ahead of me. To the family I was mopey, grumpy, and uncommunicative. It was an unnecessary use of the cold shoulder, although I merely felt detached and sleepy. It all helps to describe the way in which I developed a feeling of being on my own.

Despite all the sleepless nights and private thoughts, the most significant factor in the evolution of my sense of self has been my ability to manufacture the image of the golden boy.

The golden boy is a product of materialism; the foster child of ambition and illusion. He is the realization of his parents' dreams of success, and the vindication of their failures. The unfavorite favored son, more of a public phenomenon than an ontological reality. God's gift to headmasters and college admission directors.

He is a marvelous collection of attributes: intelligence, humor, athletic ability, honesty, diligence, good looks, modesty, kindness. Mostly reputation; he can do no wrong. He wins all the commencement prizes, leads every honor roll, gets invited to all the parties, and everyone calls him by his nickname. Captain of varsity teams, student council, cum laude. Interested in art, music, theatre, etc., gets the girls. You name it.

But the golden boy is never allowed to be seen as a person, to be bad or wrong, unfaithful, stupid. For he can only be what other people tell him he is, a personification of their unrealized ideals. Teacher's Pet, mother's little helper, Brown-nose, call him what you will. The golden boy is a clay pigeon. A silver picture frame. A plastic comic book hero. He's a lousy piece of propaganda. Transparent. He's been pimped. Above all, he's lonely.

I have sought this person eagerly, relentlessly, and I have tried to repudiate it. Both at the same time. A lot of it just was, I could not escape it. Now, I am trying not to fight it, merely to do without it. I wonder if that is possible, since it is such a direct manifestation of daddyism. But until I allow myself an identity outside the realm of the golden boy, I don't think I could do without this deadly reassurance from the past. But no matter how hard I tried to be seen for myself, I couldn't make people see through those phony attributes. I could talk my way in or out of anything without saying a word, because they lis-

tened to my record, evaluated my image be.
met them. They didn't give me a chance to
honest. By the time I was a sophomore in s
knew that the values I may have represented
direct relation to the value of me as a pers
only a form, a model, a structure. The only
could stop people from relating only to my app
my clothes, was to rebel against the golden boy
would have been just as much society's trap as
mer. This perception that public rewards were a
ficial and often fraudulent was the third great lesson of my life. It was driven home to me year after year. The second greatest lesson was the knowledge that I had this strange power over people.

The biggest lesson of all, though, was that I was so terribly afraid of power. When I was three I slammed my sister's finger in the door, and she almost lost it (she was one year old). I remember watching the blood run down the drain as my mother held her cracked finger under the cold water. I knew I hadn't done anything wrong, but I also knew that all the pain and screaming and confusion was due to something I had done. I had done nothing and yet everything; and I realized that I couldn't call back my action. My only thought was to make sure I could control this dangerous power in the future.

The association of the power of the golden boy to the primitive power of the innocent child is undeniable. As I grew more and more conscious of the deep jealousy and resentment in my closest friends, I began to fight against the whole syndrome. Once I saw that golden boy equalled power, I began to tie my hands behind my back.

So it was an absolutely profound realization that the golden boy routine had originally been a subconscious defense against the threat of unconscious aggression. In order to protect myself against the accidental unleashing of power, which had proved so harmful when I slammed my sister's finger in the door, I was determined to be the ultimate good child, or golden boy. Because if you did everything right, and lived up to mommy and daddy's best expectations, then you were automatically nice, and by some weird psychological definition, "harmless." Never do anything wrong (i.e. hurt people) meant never get in a situation where you might exert your will independently. Be "good" meant: use their mechanisms for control;

he best meant: you are the most peaceful. le did I know what other powers I was so earnestly eveloping.

While this fear of power may have originated after the incident with my sister, I believe it was crucially, pitifully solidified in the death of my father. Over the last three years I have become convinced that as a four year-old child I believed the illusion that I killed my father. At any rate, a part of me was sympathetic to his loss. But the part of me which so depended on his company and his love looked in utter horror at my supposed complicity in the event. The impact of those two colliding forces at such an early age generated such guilt and such repression that I did not uncover their sources till I was twenty-one.

In the shadow of this discovery of the origin of my fear of power, it is possible to understand how a great deal of the motivation for the will to golden boy lies in my conscious obligation to my father. Not only did I use this role as a means of escape from the responsibilities of power, but I needed exactly such an instrument to atone for my guilt. The remarkable thing is that I was so well suited for the role. Surely I would have found another means had I not been so capable, but the neurosis might have revealed itself sooner. I am still confounded by this guilt-ridden compulsion which has tyrannized my life for so long.

Eventually this fear of aggression permeated every mode of behavior, and suffocated each attempt to express myself. Activity of any form became associated with that primordial power where one is unable to tolerate the act, and must therefore refuse the violence. My life has been at the mercy of this brutally strict super-ego which has myself as my father punishing me for horrible deeds, and preventing me from executing further atrocities.

At Harvard I suddenly found that I could not allow myself to succeed in any area. Somehow papers grew to be associated with power, with the golden boy, with playing their games, with trying to do the best for daddy. Intelligence was power, sports was power, grades and graduate schools was power. I wasn't even allowed to get interested in any outside activity.

Sophomore year I took a Shakespeare course because

I really dug Shakespeare. Soon I couldn't read the plays. I would sit down to enjoy just two hours of reading, and find that I couldn't turn pages. It was ridiculous, it infuriated me, but the more determined I was, the more I would drift into a state of suspended animation.

Last year as a junior I took a photography course at the Visual Arts Center. As soon as I found myself turned on to the medium, and after I decided that I was doing some good work, I had to cut myself off. I was unable to work on the final project which covered half the term.

Any glimmer of life was a threat. I had to remain cool, dead, in order to assure my super-ego that I was weak and helpless. The subconscious forces are strong. They keep me glued at dead center, unable to move an inch towards any extreme. I am fogbound, unconscious, trouble-free. Doped. The narcotic existence. I am not able to validate any experience.

My fear of success grew so strong that I had to seek failure. The most extreme example is my relation to the Natural Sciences requirement. For the past two years I have enrolled in a Nat Sci course with the subconscious knowledge that I would do no work. NO work. NONE, except to go to most of the lectures which was a ritual to keep me oblivious to my condition, I didn't even try to do the homework or the papers. On the exams I took a smug pleasure in drawing pictures. And the worst thing is that I could never worry about it. The thought of not graduating, of having to take two extra courses, of summer school, never phased me. It was a fierce neurotic reaction, an absolute psychological prerequisite. Frontal lobotomy. I had sought failure before, but in this case, I was determined.

This reaction is a reaction out of fear, a reaction out of guilt. It is a defensive reaction and a helpless reaction. It is aggression turned inwards, cruel self-persecution. Self-hate. Hate against the self which would act, will, drive, do, express. It is the most severe punishment in the world.

It is also a weak, tortured expression of hate by that same self against the father, against the motivation for guilt. It is a sickly attempt to break away from paralysis. Negative identity. Failing. I rebuke the father which would have me succeed; I spite his power. Yet a pawn of his authority, still a servant to his awesome strength, I am quietly denying him my life. He can't have it, although he has taken mine. I am castrated, I offer him only death. It is my only way of getting back at him, of not wholly abiding that treacherous sense of guilt. I am still a captive, still dead. It is an enormous sacrifice.

I still suck my thumb, and I hate death. The thumb stands for my weakness, my inability to overcome it. I am afraid of death. I am afraid of it like I was afraid to move into the room our maid had, the one who died in our kitchen. Like I was afraid, for years, to think of my father's death. I am afraid to think that the only relief from my guilt over his death can come from the ultimate psychological resolution of the desire to get back to him, to absolve myself, in pure relation: to join him in death. I am afraid that what the Ouija board spelled out to me, that I would die when I was twenty-five, is true. I am afraid of my own power over myself, afraid of my father in me as death, afraid that guilt will seize my life. I hate death like I hate the father who won't let me use the force I need not to be afraid.

I am afraid of aggression, I am afraid of what will happen if I lose control. Somewhere in my head aggressive thoughts killed my father; the will came from the desire to have my mother all to myself. His death scared me from any such will in the future; I am afraid of my mother's implicit challenge to step forward and take his place. So I suck my thumb, am a nice boy, passive. I wouldn't hurt anyone.

My father has entirely blocked up my aggressive mode. The monstrous guilt prevents freedom inaction. I feel I owe it to him to be like him, to succeed for him, for the sake of him. I can't ever allow myself to equal him or follow him. I hate him for dominating my life, yet all he ever did was love me. I must kill the father, but I have already done so and regretted it. All this is me, and then none of me. It is a tremendous sacrifice. Unrewarded. I offer one unreality here and there, Nat Sci, in order to preserve the higher morality, the supreme priority which is my debt, my guilt, to my father. One sacrifice satisfies the neurosis temporarily, keeps the monster from wholly eating me up. I must gain back the will to power.

Chapter 9

Attitudes and Reactions Evoked by a Suicide

Robert Albert, Jr.

"It was just a beautiful thing that I could tell him to his face what was wrong with his course and we did something about it. It really worked out, and there were good vibrations, and he called me tonight to thank me, and it was important to me that I was in a position to say that you don't have to thank me, Peter." This quote is from a letter my roommate Robert wrote to his fiancee. It refers to his tutor and friend, Dr. Peter Ball, a young Assistant Professor at one of Harvard's professional schools. A week later, he shot himself in his office, just before class time.

The purpose of this paper is to examine the reactions to the suicide, and perhaps to shed some light on attitudes toward suicide and death. The material consists of two talks with Robert about the subject, two letters he wrote, and talks with three other students, one of whom had recently become a close friend of the deceased. This person, Orval, is a senior at Harvard College. Peter had gone once to a group with Orval that met weekly. In addition to this, Peter had become involved in Synanon, a community centered around the "game" of intense emotional confrontation in the group, where Orval had spent last summer and planned to return. Orval had visited the Ball's home on various occasions and over the previous two months had gotten to be good friends with Peter and his wife. Robert was also a participant in the weekly group meetings that Peter and Orval were involved in. He was in Peter's tutorial, which Orval audited. As indicated in the quotation at the beginning of this paper, Robert had begun to play a significant role in the tutorial with Peter. Robert, myself, and the other two students referred to, Bill and Henry are all juniors at Harvard College and roommates. Only Robert and Orval knew Peter personally.

I spoke to Robert about his reactions to the suicide

the day after it occurred. In addition to this, he gave me a letter written to his fiancee the night of the event. We talked about his feelings again six weeks afterwards. My own feelings were recorded the first night I questioned Robert, and I spoke to Henry and Bill the next night, Wednesday. Orval did not care to talk two days after the suicide, the first time I approached him with the subject. He described his feelings in detail to me six weeks later.

These five students could be considered "average" Harvard students, but only in the sense that 57 is the average of 83 and 31. None of them believes in an afterlife or adheres to any religion. Suicide is not held to be an immoral act by them.

The predominant initial reaction was shock. Robert and Orval were in tutorial waiting for Peter who was late. The head tutor came in and someone asked where Peter was. The man replied that Dr. Ball had just committed suicide. The immediate response was disbelief, the refusal to accept the painful reality. Robert said, "Would you repeat that, please?" After reassertion of the fact, the response was stunned silence. Robert said he was freaked out and did not know how to react or what to say. He soon sought the comfort of others. Orval was shocked, confused, and angry, and wanted to be alone. Bill and I had just gotten stoned. Both of us were stunned and did not know how to react. We were also somewhat resentful of being brought down. I was concerned about how I ought to act, thinking that above all I must act serious.

These reactions of shock and confusion are significant. Parsons and Lidz (1967) describe a change in American orientation toward death that puts these reactions in perspective. The orientation toward death is part of a larger orientation which Parsons and Lidz refer to as instrumental activism. This involves a desire to extend control over the environment and to adopt a pragmatic outlook. The manifestations of this orientation can be seen in the premium placed on technological advancement and the high value accorded to material wealth in America. According to Parsons and Lidz this orientation has resulted in the modern development of a pattern for valuing prolongation of life and rationalized schema for identifying controllable components of the death complex. Death is inevitable, but death at early age can be prevented. Mainly through progress in the field of medicine, death control has been established so that death in early age, say before sixty, is unusual. The general orientation described also involves an accent on youth and productivity. Thus deaths of younger people are unexpected and especially disturbing to modern Americans. This is particularly true of the case in question, where the deceased was an extremely productive and quite young member of society. In speaking to me, Robert said that "It was hard to think of someone dying who is young." A great deal of the shock experienced here was due to this unexpected nature of the death.

The students stressed their confusion and not knowing what to do or think. The aspect of unexpectedness in the death as discussed above contributed to this feeling. The situation was a very foreign one which these men were not prepared to handle. I felt some degree of anxiety or pressure to react in some way, but simply had no standard or preparation from which to act. There appears to be little discussion and information concerning suicide and death in America. The orientation toward instrumental activism results in a separation of the controllable components of the death complex from the inevitable components, which are ignored. The attitude would be that the inevitability of death (at old age) is a fact and there is no use talking or thinking about it. As a result, when a death occurs, particularly of unexpected nature, there is no pattern of behavior to draw upon, and confusion results.

In observing people's reactions to the dead person, I noticed that tied in with the shock and bewilderment was a certain fear and respect for the topic. I personally felt that anything that might be said would be trivial, too light, or morbid. What was said was uncomfortable. Orval resented it if the subject was taken other than very seriously. Henry said he had wondered how Peter had killed himself and if he had left a note, but he did not ask. Neither Orval nor Robert actively sought out information about the circumstances of Peter's death, not finding out until such information was volunteered. The general attitude toward the topic of death involves respect and a sense of sanctity. There is a very definite tendency to idealize a person after he is dead. The national behavior after the death of John F. Kennedy is an excellent example of this tendency. There prevails an attitude that now that he is dead we must do the best we can by him. Present day funeral orations and obituaries usually consist of listing the achievements of the deceased and glorifying them. Possibly this is a development from religion, where a man had to be evaluated in terms of his character on the question of whether he would make it to heaven or not. Also there is at least in part a personal identification process with each person hoping that he himself will be remembered in a favorable light after he dies, with some kind of positive immortality. At any rate there remains some sacredness to death, perhaps carried over from primitive times. This is in spite of the secularization of death due to the development and spread of ideas on evolution and other aspects of modern thought such as psychology. No doubt death is still viewed with some awe and fear because of its unknown nature.

Grief played very different roles for Orval and Robert. Orval did not speak much or exhibit overt behavior about Peter's death for the first two days. He felt that he was carrying a burden inside of himself. Two days later, at a meeting with a group he let out his emotions and cried violently. Afterward he felt as if the burden had been removed. He achieved a short range resolution, and only the long range resolution remained. On the other hand, Robert showed no release of emotions. It was not as necessary for him, as Orval was much closer to Peter. Instead, Robert dealt with the problem on an intellectual plane. He showed no grief but rather concern and mental turmoil. Henry, who is very close to Robert, said that he wanted him to talk about his personal emotional loss because that was the only real factor. He did not press the issue at all and it was never faced. Robert would only say, "He doesn't exist any more." Robert managed to avoid the grief and tried to forget, playing pool and getting stoned. Two tendencies come up here, which I feel are dangerous. Both result in avoiding emotional release. The search for rationality of Western man results in intellectualization of problems, denying the emotions. Tensions are not released. This we see in Robert, who denied himself the resolution which Orval found. The other way is simple deprivation of release through the value of "being strong" or "stiff upper lip." This is just another way of denying the realities at hand.

A point of great concern in this suicide are the clues to the suicide. Robert wrote: "Peter was a man I was just getting into and Orval was really beginning to be close to him, and neither of us as sensitive people could sense how desperate he must have been." Neither Robert nor Orval had any idea at all that the man was near suicide. Both experienced feelings of guilt and fear that they were involved. Orval chastised himself for not knowing what was going on and not helping. He felt that Dr. Ball had remained behind the barrier of authority and the class had accepted the bluff, not forcing a more real relationship. Nevertheless as a close friend of Peter's he had seen no indication forecasting the suicide. Robert had seen the man as very much in control of his life and successful. He saw him as healthy in that Peter was supposed to know of the psychological forces controlling men. In retrospect it appears that there were some very minor clues. Peter was seeing a psychoanalyst, who also had no premonition of the suicide. Mrs. Ball, who had similar interests to her husband, also did not have any idea of her husband's plight. Yet Robert points out it could not have been on the spur of the moment, since Peter had a gun in his office. Apparently the root of the problem was Peter's work at the school. He was alienated from the people there. Students disliked his teaching methods and his foreign ideas. The suicide note he left indicated confusion, disappointment, and disillusionment. The clues in this case were particularly subtle, making it harder to take and more shocking.

Through their experience, Robert and Orval became aware of the whole question of suicide and some of their attitudes toward it came out. Robert had not thought about suicide very much. He said he had never actually considered doing it. It was inconceivable to him. He could not conceptualize his death. If he was in a situation where he were certain of dying the next day, he conjectured, he would commit suicide. This would be in order to avoid dying. The suicidal act can be a final way of asserting control over one's life, and in a sense gaining immortality. Present day technology has given man the power over life and death through such means as nuclear bombs, birth control pills, and the practice of medicine. As indicated previously, this control is cherished in America, and suicide is the final way of not relinquishing that control.

Orval sees himself as a little closer to suicide than Robert does. It has occurred to him as a possibility when he has been down. Yet he did not see it as a serious possibility and finds sleep a much more satisfactory form of cessation. He views suicide as frightening, especially in the loss of control "after pulling the trigger."

When people threaten suicide, Orval's reaction is mainly one of anger. This feeling extended only in very small part to Peter. Suicide is a personal question to everyone, whether they face it or not, Orval pointed out, and this is much of the reason why it is a taboo subject and angers people. With respect to others committing suicide, Robert stressed that he has no way of thinking about it, nowhere to start. He has no rational structure with which to examine motives or look for clues.

The indications of all this, I feel, are clear. There is a lack of information in America concerning suicide and death. People need to be more aware of death so that they can cope with it when it comes. The uncontrollable aspects of the death complex must not be ignored. People must be brought to think about the nature of death and encouraged to develop a pattern of response to it. A realization that death is not separate from living, but part of living, should be inculcated. Death at early age would not be so unexpected and perhaps could be prevented more efficiently if it were not a source of shock and fear. Research on suicide and death and grief should be encouraged. Hopefully, psychological research would aid in the development of a satisfactory response pattern to death. The outlet of emotion which was so helpful to Orval would be seen in a highly favorable rather than unfavorable light. Suicide is a question which must be posed to more and more people. It is a much larger problem than most people realize. If people think about suicide in the present, when they are rational and can develop proper perspectives, they will be much better prepared to handle the problem satisfactorily in times of stress and greater irrationality. As in Robert's case, people have no knowledge of clues to suicide in others. If this information were spread, productive lives could be saved. Human understanding and concern is the most effective weapon against suicide. The greatest need is to deepen the awareness and sensitivity of people to their fellow men.

REFERENCE

Parsons, Talcott and Lidz, Victor. Death in American Society. In E. S. Shneidman (Ed.) Essays in Self-Destruction. New York: Science House,1967.

Note: Except for the author's name, all the names in this paper have been changed.

Chapter 10

The Death Cult of James Dean

Amy F. Cooper

A study of James Dean can begin and end with a paragraph that appeared in Time on October 10, 1955, that neatly captures the essence of his violent end:

> Died. James Dean, 24, most promising young cinemactor of 1955 (East of Eden); in a collision as he sped along a darkening highway in his silver Porsche Spyder sports car to enter a road race one week after he completed work in a new film, Giant; near Paso Robles, California. September 30.

My own interest in James Dean evolved out of learning about the "cult" that sprang up among his most avid followers after his death --a cult that grew in numbers until it included the adult as well as the adolescent, the intellectual as well as the teeny-bopper. The ghostly sensations left behind by this death cult and the aura of mystery and tragedy that still surrounds the name of James Dean fascinate me. I have sought to add width and breadth to the movie magazines' cardboard cutout of the late actor. Using the psychological approaches to death we have been exploring in Social Relations 155, I have tried to show the relation of James Dean's death to his life style and personality, and I have attempted to describe and analyze the curious impact his death had on his fans. What we will be dealing with here is the phenomenon of death, both in terms of an individual's participation in his own demise and in terms of mass experiencing of a significant other's demise --in this case a movie star.

A psychological look at the way James Dean lived can lead to some conclusions as to just how "accidental" and unintentioned his early death really was, in much the same way that a "psychological autopsy" (Shneidman, 1969) may determine the degree to which a death is suicidal or accidental. And we will also consider the appropriateness of his death, using the term "appropriate death" as it has been defined by Dr. Avery Weisman. Finally, it will be necessary to look at the Dean cult as it reflects ideas of identification and the rationalization of the irrational.

A Subintentioned Death (Shneidman, 1963).

The son of a Quaker, James Dean was born and raised in Fairmount, Indiana. He had a lonely childhood, it appears, since his mother died when he was only nine years old. Dean the actor was in many respects similar to Dean the man -- rebellious, reckless, and confused. "He was spiritually lonely and tumultous, "Newsweek reports," a somber-eyed romantic who seemed to be fighting something all by himself." (June 18, 1956). Maybe this "something" was society, or maybe it was the weaker side of his own personality.

Whatever he was fighting, it seems Dean was not as sure as some other people were of his own greatness. Indeed, "walled around with suspicions of his own inadequacies and his defense against their discovery", he tended to be shy and withdrawn.

. . .I don't see how people stay in the same room with me. I know I wouldn't tolerate myself.

(James Dean, Life, September 1956)

Sanford Roth, a long-time friend of Dean's, suggests that this intensity and shyness made it difficult to know him. Roth writes that James Dean would sometimes sit for hours outside of a friend's house waiting for other visitors to leave before he would go in. (Colliers November 25, 1955).

But in the midst of this deep seriousness and severe self-questioning, Dean was extremely enthusiastic about a wide variety of interests --i.e., motorcycles, sculpturing, photography, jazz, cats, classical music, and bullfighting. Seeming never to be satisfied with just being good at many things, he pushed himself to be superior in everything he did, whether it be sportscar racing or acting. East of Eden, Giant, and Rebel Without A Cause, for example, were all made in the period of one year without respite. As Roth says;

There was so much he wanted to learn. . .once he said that even if he lived to be one hundred, there wouldn't be time for everything.

Looking at photographs of James Dean, I have been moved at different times by the sensuality, the poetic sensitivity, the little boy-lost innocence, or the practical-minded professional quality of his face. Contradictions clash--innocence with experience, passion with intellect--and, as in all of us, merge to create the totality of an individual. Dean was restless, ambitious, and ever-questing. And he was a true rebel. It is interesting to note that he always entered resturants by the back door. Such a symbolic action demonstrates his drive to question authority and repudiate conformity. Nor was Dean himself protected from this questioning; he was deeply tormented by the weaknesses and inadequacies he felt to be a part of his personality. George Stevens, who directed him in Giant, said of Dean:

All in all, it was a hell of a headache to work with him. He was always pulling and hauling, and he had developed this cultivated, designed irresponsibility. It's tough on you, he'd seem to imply, but I've just got to do it this way. . .

(Saturday Review, October 13,1955)

Inherent in James Dean's rebellious and searching personality were elements of violence directed at himself and his existence. Arthur Knight once observed that along with Dean's carefully nurtured talent for acting he was also nurturing a second talent for self-destruction. We shall consider the elements of this "second talent" in an attempt to determine the degree to which Dean may have participated in his own death.

One of the late actor's favorite tricks involved the making of a hangman's noose which he then tied tightly around his own neck. The trick was so popular and performed so often that he had a noose permanently hanging in his living-room. Such humor borders on the macabre. One also wonders what caused Dean to quit jobs in the way he did. After a quarrel with a director he once walked out and another time he quit a show in two weeks after a quarrel with the producer. Playing with a hangman's noose is not in itself an act of violence, nor is walking out of a studio in itself

self-destructive. But both behavior patterns indicate a reckless disregard for self and an attitude of defiance toward security. There is also a hint of playing with or teasing death. They are in fact patterns of behavior comparable in significance to the rebellious abandon with which Dean as a troubled youth in Rebel Without A Cause chicken races with another boy along the edge of a cliff.

James Dean did not die so young or so violently because he quit jobs or played with a hangman's knot. But the same defiant recklessness characteristic of these acts shows up again in his love of sports cars and speed. He always drove over the speed limit. And he said there could be no better way to die than in sports-car racing. The night Dean collided with another car on the way to the Salinas auto races, he was driving excessively fast. Hastening his own demise? There is, of course, greater chance that death will come sooner when you drive fast than when you drive carefully and obey the rules. Disobeying the rules of the road, it seems, was but one part of James Dean's disobedience of the rules of society, and finally the risks involved in both counts caught up with him.

Shneidman (1963) defined a subintentional death as one in which the decedent plays a covert, sublimal, unconscious role in hastening his own demise. In his reckless disregard for security and his death-daring, as demonstrated by quitting jobs, making jokes about hanging, and driving at excessive speeds, James Dean would appear to have played a greater part in his death than the official certification of "Accident" implies.

An Appropriate Death (Weisman, 1970)

Dean's violent end at the age of twenty-four would have been a fitting fate for any of the characters he portrayed on the screen. Jett Rink, the character Dean played in Giant (with Elizabeth Taylor and Rock Hudson), met an end similar in its impact to the actor's. A poor ranch employee who is at one time madly in love with Miss Taylor, Rink strikes it rich on a supposedly worthless piece of land and becomes a fabulous oil millionaire. After he makes his money, however, he turns arrogant, vulgar, sodden, and pitiable. Eventually, Rink kills himself by jumping off a porch -- shouting that no one is going to take his money away. (Life, April 1956). He defies society by killing himself; before anyone can make him poor again, Rink dies in the midst of his wealth. It is not difficult to conclude that Jett Rink dies the way he has lived. He has always been arrogant and willful, and in committing suicide he expresses still more arrogance and a determination to do himself in before someone else does.

Weisman defined "appropriate death" in terms of compatability with ego identity and consummation of a wish to die in a certain way. An individual dies appropriately when his dying and death follows the way he and others feel he should or would like to die. First of all, there is an appropriateness of time in Dean's death:

> If he had lived, he'd never have been able to live up to his publicity.
>
> Humphrey Bogart (Life, September 24, 1956)

It is true that Dean died just as he was rising as a movie star--two of the three films he made were released posthumously. And in Hollywood there is always the uneasy question of how great the next movie will be or how soon the fans will start flocking to something new, especially when you are considering the fickle loyalties of adolescent idol-worshippers.

Furthermore, there is the appropriateness of the way Dean died. On the screen Dean communicated best through the violence of speeding motorcycles and hot-rods. Like Marlon Brando in The Wild One, he seemed engaged in an heroic lifetime fight against established systems of behavior. He was once asked whether he thought sports-car racing was too dangerous, and he replied, "What better way to die?" After this comment, it is fitting that James Dean died in his Porsche Spyder on the way to the auto races in Salinas.

Dean died in what should have been the midst of his career and in the midst of his life experience. For no matter how inner-tormented he might have been, no matter how driven and searching his spirit, he was very much in the midst of life. Dean was always trying to improve his own offering to life and his wide variety of interests in music, art, sports, and animals suggest an enthusiastic awareness of what living has to offer. There is no doubt that Dean's reckless attitude toward security and safety may have played a covert role in hastening his death. But his death was an "appropriate" one; he died as he had tried to live--swiftly, passionately, and in full rebellion against authority.

The Cult of James Dean

The Dean cult was born on the day of Dean's death. Immediately after the accident, fan magazines began exhausting all sources, real and imagined, for new information about his life. Even a sports-car publication got into the act by publishing an article entitled: "A Great Actor Was on the Road to Becoming a Great Driver When Death Released His Heavy Foot from the Throttle." (Life, Sept. 1956). The funeral in his home town of Fairmount attracted more than the total 2,700 population of the community. Eleven months later, Dean ranked Number 1 in Photoplay's actor popularity poll, and drew 1,000 fan letters a week, far exceeding the amount of fan mail he got while alive. Girls sent in asking for a picture, a piece of hair, or a piece of the smashed car. There was a rumor that the car had been stolen in the night and that pieces were being sold for outrageous sums, but in fact the wreckage of the Porsche was bought for $1000 by a Dr. Eschrich of Burbank, California, who wanted the shattered thing simply to get the motor for his own racing car.

The public went "necrophiliac" when Dean died. Newsracks were full of special issues consisting only of pictures of Dean relaxing--wearing blue jeans or posing unshaven with his sports-car. And everywhere there was a hint of surrealism and mysticism in connection with this spontaneous death cult. It seemed especially ghoulish that loyal fans, for the sum of $5.00, could purchase life-size molded faces of the actor, supposedly made out of a plastic material that felt like human skin.

Dean had dated Maila Nurmi, an actress several years older than himself, who played Vampira on television. After the accident, there was talk of her having caused his death through black magic. Furthermore, Miss Nurmi admitted to be in frequent communication through the veil with the departed Dean. After that, for a small sum of money, spiritualists all over the United States would get fans into contact with their deceased hero. An air of darker things beyond influenced the type of cult behavior that emerged with Dean's death.

What does it all mean -- this seemingly morbid fascination with death, these attempts to preserve in this world the personality as well as the memory of a young actor? Two points are important in an analysis of the strong emotional reaction caused by James Dean's death: ego-identification and the mystery of death. Several authors have pointed out that many young people strongly identified with the rebellious character Dean portrayed on and off the screen. He was in a sense "everybody's adolescent" -- an individual not yet sure of his own identity and even less sure of the standards of the society around him. James Dean was much like the boy he portrayed in Rebel Without A Cause; a boy who was basically good, but who got into trouble because he found it difficult to conform to his environment, and who suffered greatly from a lack of parental love and guidance. That James Dean was of youth and for youth is seen in a poignant letter to the Editors of Life, October 15, 1956:

" To us teenagers, Dean was a symbol of the fight to make a niche for ourselves in the world of adults." Something in us that is being sat on by convention and held down was, in Dean, free for all the world to see.

He was, therefore, a symbol to many of youth's battle in the adult world. But symbols know not time and space; symbols are without beginning or end, and as made clear on September 30, 1955, Dean was not. Cult images, such as photographs and molded heads, are much more expressions of the abstract concepts of freedom and youth James Dean stood for than representations of the late actor. And the strong public reaction to his death may well have been an attempt to keep the symbol of Dean alive.

For James Dean's immortality lies in terms of what youth saw him to be. His death was so tragic, so violent, and yet so appropriate that many young people viewed it as an hero's end. He was the champion of their cause, and he died not only in the midst of life at twenty-four, but also in the midst of rebellion against conformity, communicating to the last through speed and shiny cars. "When James Dean was killed in that horrible accident," wrote one fan, "it seemed like a big, black curtain had been drawn in my life. But he will never die, no, not the great James Dean. He can't." (Life, September 24, 1956). Perhaps Dean cannot die because what was in him is in the world -- youth, questions, and rebellion.

The comment "He can't." in the above letter brings up the second element to be considered in relation to the curious death cult springing up after the actor's death. Death is a most mysterious thing; something which even if we accept as inevitable escapes rationality. The idea of non-being or being in a different sense than we are now is incomprehensible and frightening. Especially when you are an adolescent, just beginning to experience life, it is troubling and mystifying to learn that you will end. And it is equally difficult to accept the cessation of another individual, especially when that individual is a movie actor with whom so many young people identified.

This unwillingness to accept the death of someone as notable as James Dean may have influenced the creation of a wide-spread rumor that Dean had not died in the auto crash, but had been so badly disfigured that he was forced against his will to spend the rest of his life in a private institution. And there were also whispers of reincarnation and resurrection.

We have a choice of ways with which to deal with death. We can either refuse to accept its reality or we may fashion it into some rational, tangible terms that can be understood. Both ways retard the realization of finality. James Dean as a movie star and public figure was super-realistic, somehow above the world, and to many fans immortal. The rumors of reincarnation and the sincere assertions that he was not dead seem in part a refusal to accept his mortality. And the mystical cult growing up, complete with iconography and high priests, may indeed represent an attempt to preserve the symbolic significance of Dean's life, and an attempt to deal with the mystery of death in tangible terms.

Malinowski defined magic as man's attempt to control that over which he had no control. Spiritualists, transference of a dead man's spirit into the body of a living man, and plastic likenesses made of a flesh-like material would all seem magical means of controlling death. "We don't consider ourselves morbid", one female fan wrote, "It's just that Jimmy Dean was so brilliant and death is so hard to understand." Not being able to understand death on its own terms, it becomes necessary to deal with it in terms which man has created and can control. Abstracts like non-being become concrete communications to the beyond, and that which was unreal gains a semblance of reality.

The accident on the road to Salinas in which Dean was killed was not the beginning and the end of his involvement with death. His reckless and persistent disregard for rules and security, coupled with a feeling of taunting death with hangman's nooses and fast cars, can lead one to believe that James Dean played a role in his own early death, that certain covert elements in his personality hastened his demise. Once we begin to add dimensions like participation or subintention to the dimensionless void of Death, it is likely that the nature of an individual's death may find a new meaning. Dean's fatal crash was an "appropriate death." For he died as he lived and in the way he seemed to want to die. A hero's death, perhaps, but a very special kind of heroism. And the reactions of others to his death must be considered. Death is a mystery; if we are unable to accept its inexplicable terms, we may try to deny its reality or try to surround it with a magical atmosphere that can be manipulated. Whatever, we must do something with death. For like James Dean, the involvement of each individual with his own death is a process that begins early in his own life and continues through the lives of others.

References

"The Late James Dean." Collier's, Vol. 136, November 25, 1955.

"Moody New Star." Life, March 7, 1955.

"Delirium over Dead Star." Life, Vol. 41, September 24, 1956.

"New Lost Generation." New Republic, Vol. 136, February 4, 1957.

New Statesman, December 21, 1957.

"Stars That Won't Dim." Newsweek, June 18, 1956.

"It's Dean, Dean, Dean." *Saturday Review*, Vol. 39, October 13, 1956.

"Celluloid Monument." *Saturday Review*, Vol. 40, August 3, 1957.

Shneidman, Edwin S. Orientations towards Death: A Vital Aspect of the Study of Lives. In Robert W. White (Ed.), *Study of Lives*. New York: Atherton Press, 1963; reprinted in *International Journal of Psychiatry*, 1966, 2, 167-200; and in Shneidman, E. S., Farberow, N. L., and R. E. Litman, *Psychology of Suicide*, New York: Science House, 1970. Pp. 3-32.

Shneidman, Edwin S. Suicide, Lethality and the Psychological Autopsy. In Shneidman, E. S. and M. Ortega (Eds.), *Aspects of Depression*. Boston: Little, Brown, 1969. (*International Psychiatry Clinics*, Vol. 6, No. 2, 1969).

Weisman, Avery D. Appropriate Death. In Shneidman, E. S., Farberow, N. L., and R. E. Litman, *Psychology of Suicide*. New York: Science House, 1970. Pp. 33-36.

PART IV

PERSONAL REFLECTIONS ABOUT SELF-DESTRUCTION

Chapter 11

manny rap

Ward Abronski

works.always carry them with you,you know man. my works theyre like the eyedropper kind,not a syringe. too much hassle with the glass and all.little plastic eyedropper with a rubber bulb fitted over one end and the point over the other.i know this drug store in new york you know,like there're so many junkies in the area that they sell the eyedroppers with the bulb allready on.find your own point though.not too hard to find a cat,he's a diabetic or something,got an rx for points.or some cat works in a hospital.thats how i got mine.frank,this big spade,cleans up an shit,gets em for me.dont know how,maybe hes got a key or something, balls one of the nurses,dig?i dont know.at least i got my own.when i started shooting i used alfs works which is stupid because you can catch hep or the clap or just about any thing from someone elses.we used to sit up stairs in the bathroom of his building and shoot up. thats where his stash was.i was afraid at first because i was allways afraid of needles wether the cat on the other end of it was a docter or a junkie.but i really wanted to get high so i said to alf you hit me man cause im scared to do it myself i might fuck up, you know.so he said cool and so the first time i got hit it was by alf with his stuff and his works.he hit me good and clean too cause i really got off. shooting ups not too complicated you know its like pretty easy once you do it a few times.once you cook up your shit and get it drawn up you got your arm tied off so those veins buldge out nice and fat.then you just pick a vein and slide it right in.if you hit good a little blood shoots up like it was a string an then blossoms out. then you tap on the bulb easy getting the shit out. after you shot like about maybe a third or so you draw some of it back up.if its pink an theres blood then you still got the vein an everythings cool.this is called checking.then you keep tapping until you got it all,loosen your tie-off an she comes on like a motherfucker,when you first shoot its easy cause those veins are soft and waiting.after a while though they get hard and a point will slide right around them.then you got to probe around you know and find one.some times they collapse on you and you got to find another.some reason everybodys got his own particular spot.veins all over the place,they stick to the elbow,sometimes one special spot on a special vein till it gives out. this one cat bill hes got like a hole in his arm,little scab on it he shoots right through till it died on him. some cats use up everything,shoot right in the neck or the base of their spine.really a bummer to watch you know?

alfs dead now.he was a smooth cat you know? he was smooth but he was real crazy like.one time my man was driving out in new mexico or some place like that, he used to deal alot an he had some acid he was running for some big man in the car.alf never did any of that shit.would have just fucked him up and sure wouldnt have done much for his monkey.he used to carry it though an some other things too for the big man.the cat used to pay alf off in pure H.cut twelve to one.thats gold you know,like impossible to get.most of the shit you get on the street is five to one,four to one you know, really cut.anyway one of his headlights is out or something so this small town cop stops him.real wyatt erp type you know with the drawl an everything.so the cop stops him and as hes giving him the lecture he spots the stash.couple of thousand caps in a five gallon jar. whats that he says.so alf picks up the jar and takes one out,pops it down his mouth.nothin man,just vitamins here,try one.so old ass breath gobbles one down an then they sit around talking,with the cop who knows from nothing waiting for something to happen.twenty minutes later and all is cool so alf smiles,says goodbye an drives off.smooth,you dig? only thing is he got maybe too smooth.im not sure exactly what happened, maybe he was holding back on the man or maybe the man got up one morning pissed off or something you know. anyway one day alf cops a hot shot.not pure H,pure strychnine.looks and tasts like dope so its hard to tell.i found him with the clotted blood in his works, blue arm,the whole bit.you know,real dead.colder than a witches tit and with the worst look i ever seen on his face.i snuck out of his room an down to the street to a pay phone to tip off the cops cause i didnt want to get him being dead hung on me.so they came an found him there slumped over the table in his room.

i still think about alf once in a while you know. after all,we were pretty tight.he turned me on for the first time.i dont really know wether i should hate him for that or what but still he was only trying to help me get high like i wanted.he was doing me a favor the way we saw it then.we were pretty tight.we used to cop together from jonny.johnnys this really old cat,must be sixty,sixty five.really gross old bastard too,nasty looking you know?he had one of his ears bitten off in a fight a long time ago so there was just this fold around a hole in the side of his head.hes probably been strung out for twenty years or so and he looks it.his skins sort of see through yellow so that it looks like it should come off in his hand when he scratches or something,an somehow he looks bloated like a stiff and thin and boney at the same time.he dont have any eyebrows either,dont know what happened to them,so that his muddy eyes look out at you from inside this dirty old man fish face.an hes all the time slobbering and drooling when he talks.he should be dead too but hes not.just stands there on the corner like a zombie till a hungry junkie comes up to cop an then he stirs a little and crokes an the cop is over.then he just stands on the corner and stares at the traffic light all day like he can control it or something.he pays off the heat so they dont bother him and nobody rolls him cause hes been around so long that its considered bad luck to do it cause he always lays a bag or two on you when its down on you and you dont have any bread.

thats about the worst thing that can happen,you know? being sick an not being able to cop.sometimes its cause you dont have the bread which isnt too bad cause theres lots of ways to get bread.i deal a little sometimes cause thats the easiest way.just cut a little out for yourself before you bag it.then when you sell it you got your fix an the bread.sometimes though its because you cant find the man.or because hes late.all you do is wait.in the bick with the dirty walls an the shitty food an the cripples behind the counter an all the night riders floating in an out all the time.or on street corners.which isnt so bad in the summer except for the fact your sick.in the winter though its different.six cats hangin on to one corner at two ina morning an its five,ten degrees out.so you shiver an jump around and freeze on top of your sick.an right across the street on the other corner theres six more cats.the cops are hip somethings funny so they chase you away.when you lucky though you get to stand a couple a hours for some dinky little cat to come up with not enough bags most of the time to feed all the monkeys you know?so theres a big hassle an if you get real lucky you score.thats really the only gig that matters.a score.you got to make it then or you dont make it you know?junkiesll do anything to score man. if it means stealing or killing or lying or taking shit or sucking the junkmans cock.it dont make any difference dig cause you got to score.otherwise you get sick baby,real sick,you know?

getting sick is hell thats all man.the bible is full of shit let me tell you.hell isnt some place down in the ground where you burn up man,hell is right here up in your own room when its down on you an your alive an on fire an you got cramp in your legs like theyre going to turn in on themselves. inside of you is like inside a volcano or something.you know its so fucking hot.so you eat ice cubes right?by the tray full man. ever try to swallow an ice cube whole? it dont fit so good let me tell you.especially with the cramps.your throat close up on you so much you cant even swallow the spit you dont have but your so crazy you got to eat that ice cube now!you know?so you try to force it down an it gets stuck there like a hot blade inside you an now you cant breath an your choking so you try to scream because of the cramps an your burning up an your choking an your gonna die,you know?only your so hot it starts to melt fast and starts sliding down real slow like.you still cant breath for a while but it finaly gets there an then you can.only when it does get there it doesnt make any difference cause nothings gonna put out that fire except a shot.so you roll a-round in the wet bed and wish to christ you could get a taste of something or at least die,but you cant and you dont.your soaked through you know cause you sweat like a motherfucker.all over you know?it runs in your eyes an stings an its the only way you can keep your mouth wet.the sheets get like you could wring them out. theyre wet from more than just the sweat too.you puke alot you know an most of the time you make it over the side of the bed but not always.that stops after a while though cause youve only got so much in your stomach right?then you just get the dry heavs which is maybe not so bad cause you stop getting it on you an maybe worse cause with the cramps an all sometimes they last ten minutes or so without letting up.then theres the shit.you roll aroun in your own shit.dig,all the time your shooting man you hardly ever take a shit,once in a while but most of the time not you know?its the junk that does it.not exactly sure what happens but it does something to you.they give you paregoric when you got diarrhea,opium must have something to do with it.i dont know.anyway,when its down on you and you cant get the junk your guts make up for lost time.you try to fight it but you cant stop the cramps you know,so it just comes.so all the time your twitching an shit you roll all over an it just keeps coming an the bed gets wetter an all an you keep sweating an puking an rolling around in it an you feel lower than a fuckin animal but theres nothing you can do about it.its not so bad though when your room or maybe some other cats room.the trouble comes when your locked up you know? some ass hole copy busts you for something and they take you to night court and then to the tombs dig? thats where they throw all the junkies and alkies you know the bums,derelicts and all.you make it there and first thing you get searched and you got to take a shower which is the biggest joke cause thats the fil-thest place i ever saw.then you go an see the doctor right an he looks at you sees your strung out an says, just lie down an get plenty of rest.like you had a choice you know?so then you go an you get your cell. at first they put two cats in a cell.one on the bed one on the floor.the beds just springs dig,so if you want to make it you got to put your blanket under you instead of over you which is a bitch if its winter an its cold.if your cool though you take the floor cause you know your gonna be sick an when you start you could twitch yourself right of the bed and land on the con-creat.i seen it happen.later they stick more cats in. usually theres at least five in a cell-one on the floor, one on the bed,one under the bed,one on the table where they stick the food,an one on the can.its nothing for them to cram more in though.on friday nights when they make their big sweep through the east side,forsyth streetpark an christie street an the bowery they got all the cells on the drunks side of the floor filled so they cram them in with us you know that means youve got a couple of sick junkies crawling around and two or three cats screamin with the DTs in the same cell. they get a better break too cause that old bastard of a doctor will give them some thing to knock them out. a junkie cant even get a fucking asprin you know?just lie there an be sick an watch the crazy drunks and the mice running around.

with all that you wonder why you dont kick right? ive tried a couple a times but that dont mean shit, you know?i mean junkies theyre all the time quitting. but they never do.some of them try to cold turkey. you know,real crazy.ive had to cold turkey twice an i sure wouldnt chose it.other ways to do it you go to a hospital or something.not much better.they got all kinds of programs,doctors an nurses an shit but nothing really works.i mean they can clean out your veins sometimes but they can never clean out your head.ive been clean a few times,detoxifed they call it,an made promises an sworn id never look at shit again but as soon as you hit the streets man you get the old butterflys back you know?you want a taste almost as bad as if you never went inside.because thats where its at for you,you know?you want to get high.you forget all about being sick an kicking an the waiting all the time an watching old junkies slobber an drool over their dope an thinking youll be like that some day ha-ha an pushing it out of your mind cause you know you will be an dead friends like alf or danny an pietro who OD or that cat you heard about who crammed eleve bags up his ass when he was busted only that broke and the stupid shit shuffled of his mortal coil with the super hit look in his eyes,or dom who couldnt take the nagging his bitch gave him about being strung out so she found him when she came back from work with his black tounge hanging out of the red face with the ruptured blood vessles in its swollen eyes,and the stretched scrawny neck snapped like a chickens,hanging naked from the ceiling over the pile of shit his jerking muscles spewed out when he kicked away the chair an hit the end of his belt.you just want to get high man,thats all.

so you go cruisin you know?hit the street and look to score burn for that connection as much as you ever did in your life all most.cruisins almost like esp dig? i mean you got no idea where the man is but you always find him.maybe its just that he always finds you.anyway your out of the hospital and all is cool cause you feel like a stud your so clean an you can smell exaust an sweat an dirt an general street smells again after nothing but that fucking hospital disinfectant smell for so long.an you dig the traffic an all the people scurring around an the action.only way in the back of your head you dont cause you know the hospital might have been dull an painfull an all that but nobody hassled you.all they did was help even if they were so fucking smug about it.but out here you know its one big hassle an you know you cant avoid it an you know your gonna have to take shit till it comes out your ears an so you go looking for the man.cause thats how you always were baby,an thats what you are.an thats how your gonna go an you know it.you got looking for the man to feed the hungry cunt in your arm.an so instead of feeling hassled an wanting to tell everybody to fuck off you can just slide it on in an get of an nod an float away,look at your foot for eight hours an not give a shit.

or maybe this is one of the times you think you really got some balls.you want it an you know it but you dont.you hold out.you make it for a week an thats the longest youve ever held out on your own in your life.so now your really happy you know?cause you think you beat it an nobody beats it an that makes you superman,dig?but the reason you made it so far is the frenzy.like what i mean is youve been running around like a maniac all week,the routines broken,right?but when you finaly settle down an the routine starts again its something else.cats are all the time coming up an asking if you maybe want a taste or something.just a little right?nobody ever got strung on one taste did they?man when all the old bullshit starts flying at you again and you cant get away from it,that kind of talks hard to say no to.those catsll keep it up to.junkies got a funny attitude about any cats been cleaned up.its like a mixture of being happy,cuse they think,if this cat can make it i sure as hell can,an hating the bastards guts,cause they know they couldnt an worse they know he cant because nobody makes it back you know,an there sicm of this dude comin or like charles atlas or something so they try to get him back on the stuff so hell start noddin an stop flexing his new body an giving everything else a pain in the ass cause there not like that.so one day when the hassle in the air is extra thick(i can see it like some people can see smog-its yellow too)you take them up on it an push a point in the mainline.as it feels good to get high again but shitty cause your not clean any more your a junkie again only you were allways a junkie even when you were clean an you knew it.an you know you dont have any balls anyway cause they fell of the first time got hit an you havnt had a good piece of ass or been able to stop using the shit since.

thats what happened too you know?i mean you traded in one cock for another one.you got a brand new cock an it's hard silver metal.with a point.it's not part of your body any more man it rides in your pocket, waiting.an it's allways there hard and ready,dig, ready to come.thats traded too.its not your balls any more where you come man.it's your arm and your whole body an just all of you.an this comin dont go away fast.it stays with you a couple of hours at last.it rides with you an helps you real unhassled.only now when you come you really got some dues to pay.cause you know what it's costin you an you know.that that sure as hell arnt spermyou pumpin in you man it's shit, dirty cold cell sappin shit.an every time you come your killin something.an maybe pretty soon you can bring it all back home whit one huge, motherfucker you can disappear noto.an it'll be quiet,dig,really quiet.

so thats it man.an thats where im at you know? i guess where i always will be too.so you alive from one cop to the next, from cold two am fuzz hassled street corner to mens room,fag crowed urinal smell of telephone numbers on the wall to neon lit warm summer night of sickness, fell of tourists an easy bread in times square, to wet dead cold of subway station,to white towernedicsbickfordswaldorfhornanhardot tables with endless cups of coffee measuring the time hanging thickly in the sharply light night island.all to freed your monkey.the little bastard on your back an whose claws are in every cell you got an whose all the time hungry.and you dont get high any more,you know? i mean now a shot just gets you strait.an thats all. just look at the wall and rot real slow.bloat up an turn skin into yellow greay wax.an you dont give a shit about anything you know?an some cat comes along an sticks a tape-recorder in front of you an says hell pay you which means you can get a couple a more shots an like one little bit closer to being an old junkie if you talk about it in to it.so you crap out a lot a melodramatic jive an when you done you know its all-bullshit baby,thats the secret of the universe,an even that dont matter.

Chapter 12

My Suicide Attempt

and The Encouragement of Herman Hesse

Anonymous

> "Words do not express thoughts very well;everything immediately becomes a little different, a little distorted, a little foolish. And yet it also pleases me and seems right that what is of value and wisdom to one man seems nonsense to another."
>
> (Hesse, The Journey to the East,p.7)

> "Finally, he could not longer hide and contain himself. His suffering became too great, and you know that as soon as suffering becomes acute enough, one goes forward...Despair is the result of each earnest attempt to go through life with virtue, justice and understanding and to fulfill their requirements."
>
> (Hesse, The Journey to the East,p.106)

These words of Hesse relate closely to my own attempted suicide. I cannot enter into any discussion of death without some point of personal reference and no incident seems more appropriate. My attempt may now be regarded, in the perspective of three years, as analagous to Han's experiencing the "exquisite torment" of love:

> "...the pain signified that the morning peace of his life had been broken and that his soul had left that land of childhood that can never be found again."
>
> (Hesse, Under the Wheel,p.151)

I regard my suicide attempt as ultimately benevolent, despite the decided risk to life and self-estimation involved, the sapping of energy, the imposition on circumstances and plans. I have, as a result, a redefined conception of death; stated simplistically, I recognize that my fascination lay not so much with the prospect of death, as with the dramatic consequences of dying. In the tradition of courtly love, one may love his mistress, but, often enough, not his wife; insofar as removal imparts its own fascination, I can love my dying, but not my death. Likewise it is suggested of Hesse's Steppenwolf that

> "It is possible that he will learn one day to know himself. He may get hold of one of our little mirrors...He may find in one of our magic theatres the very thing that is needed to free his neglected soul. A thousand such possibilities await him."
>
> (Hesse, Steppenwolf, p.61)

One such mirror is the intimate and imminent possibility of death; such possibility is a kind of instructive dying. Like the Steppenwolf and H.H., an individual may desperately need the purgative and instructional value of attempted suicide. In my own experience, I benefitted from the impression of such negative action. Only when I had made the attempt did I sense that one cannot die and do it again; that, irrespective of any notions of immortality, I could not command the attentions of others in the state of my own non-being.

I have at various times regarded suicide as the one most active gesture in an otherwise apparently passive existence; in other words, life seemed proscribed by death, and, if any individual feels he can effect no substantial change in his life, then suicide seems an active and logical alternative. If one feels he cannot affect the nature (qualitative) of existence, then he has the option to effect the end (quantitative) of existence. Death does not seem a matter of degree; life does seem so. What Hesse suggests is what I wished I had realized prior to my attempt: that life is subtle, manifold, and perishable, that there is considerable malleability to existence, and that, given the attraction of death and self-destruction, "Instead of narrowing your world and simplifying your soul, you will at last take the whole world into your soul, cost what it may, before you are through and come to rest." (Steppenwolf, p. 71). Death is blunt (or at least I suspect so); dying is subtle (self-conception, conception of others' regarding oneself, variety in method). My thinking was materialistic, objective; I had lost faith in subjective change. Such change, I learned as a result of my action, involves the extension of oneself, the denial of an exclusively _intra_-faith; I could not with satisfaction any "longer hide and contain (myself)." Self-fulfillment seemed incompatible with the real potentialities of life; the possibility of interaction, communication, mutuality, and love seemed sufficiently remote enough to justify a self-assessment of inadequacy and ineptitude. I have since surmised that my own suicide could not be effected in the presence of others, and is certainly inconsistent with any mutual-estimations of love.

This is much the predicament of the Steppenwolf prior to this relations with Hermione and Maria. Hermione is his "mirror"; he regards and admires her, only to discover later that many of those qualities he admires reside in him also; though these qualities seem dormant, provocation and hope for self-revelation become distinct possibilities. We cannot _know_ ourselves, but may appeal to our _understanding_ of another to promote a more accurate self-estimation. Understanding implies some other-than-egocentric concern, some interrelationship. H.H. (in _The Journey to the East_) concludes that the League (life) has betrayed him, only to discover later that he has betrayed the League. Not self-inadequacy but rather impatience promotes such lack of faith. Because the League's activities are not clear in their objectives and because they are not easily definable and effable, he refuses to accept their validity. The "magic theatres" and "games" of Hesse are analagous to the unknown variations of life.

Such is the very estimation of the Steppenwolf that he regards himself as refinable to two entities: Harry and the Steppenwolf. Only after his extra-personal experiences, his discovery of love, does he sense the spontaneity and infinity of any individual. The temptation to conceive a clearly categorical view of oneself seems great. This conception may be one of morbidity, death-obsession, and suicide. Even without desperate circumstance, one may determine that a reasonable moment for self-destruction has arrived. I thought such a moment had arrived. I must try to reconstruct that moment.

The first Saturday after the first snowfall. Not too cold. Paper to be written; no interest. Roommates gone (hockey game or something); no one around. General feeling of disgust and inadequacy. No drive, no energy, no "inspiration." It's very quiet, deathly quiet. "Where's Betty?" (Old high-school friend, attractive, not very satisfying sexually, conservative, sympathetic.) Back to paper. But really, what's the purpose of de Tocqueville's view of history? First set of final examinations approaching. Not up to it. God, it's quiet. Lots of acquaintances, not so many friends. I crave attention. Call Betty. Not in. Wonder where she is. Getting depressed. Still snowing, getting colder. How could I change something? I am anything but satisfied. Why not die? i.e. why not <u>commit</u> suicide? You're going that way anyhow. Never meant to live past twenty-five. How to do it? Pills? I have got a bottle of aspirin. Why not count them. Ten little piles of five each on my desk. Looks like a possibility. Why not call Deborah (another high school friend, admires me, sort of imbalanced relationship...) and talk to her? Get attention. See if anyone is concerned, other than yourself, <u>of course.</u> (??) She's not answering either. There seems to be a conspiracy to isolate me tonight. Take the aspirin. Fifty is too many to swallow? Anyone back in room? No. Proctor is out tonight. No one to talk with. Go down hall and get a glass of water. Take twenty-five. That didn't do anything. Somewhat disappointing. Better to take the rest. Put in mouth. (God, aspirin tastes dreadful, so dry, bitter, lumpish.) Go down hall with aspirin in mouth and get water to swallow pills. Lie on bed. Not dead yet. (I suppose.) Lie still, no that's not death. Getting horribly depressed. What will they all think? Much commotion I'm certain. But still no one around. Call Betty again, but not in. Talked to operator at her college. Didn't know who she was, but good to hear a voice. Continue slow, soft, discouraging conversation. She asks if anything is strange with me? "Strange? No, what could be so strange." I talked to her about dying. What did she think of it? She keeps insisting something is wrong. I keep telling her not to worry. I thank her for her time. Give Betty the message that I called, but she won't reach me later, because time will prove all. Lie on bed fifteen minutes. Self-estimation at zero point. Don't seem to be dead yet. Still snowing. No one around. What will they think? and my parents? Betty? (Oh God, will they be sorry?) Why not go for a walk? This room is becoming oppressive. Don't care about anything. At least I won't have to write the paper now. The waiting for death is so pressing. These pills don't seem too lethal. Why not take that walk? (I leave room, no coat; walk along corridor, getting delirious; still no one around; tastes terrible; walk out into yard; the snow is so soft and so quiet; not many people in Yard tonight.) Walking very slowly to Boylston Gate. There's a Cambridge Police car. Should I say anything? What? and <u>How</u> should I say <u>it</u>? This could be embarrassing. Stare at the policemen and see if they respond. Two or three minutes later, window rolls down, "Anything wrong, fellow?" I reply, "Yes, I <u>think</u> so. You better take me to a hospital." "Hop in." Off we go through quiet, snowy Cambridge streets to Cambridge City Hospital. I wonder what the policemen think. They don't even talk to me. No curiosity. Emergency Room (not feeling well at all) seems quiet, unconcerned, no hustle about me. Doctor is calm, "What would make you do such a thing?" (God, what a ridiculous question.) They leave me alone to drink pints and pints of warm water. Every fifteen minutes or so an aide comes and asks "How're you doing?" "Fine," I reply. "Can't stay here tonight," they claim, "must go to Stillman Infirmary." They call University officials. Officials send University Police to transfer me. I wonder if I'll die. Don't especially want to, now. What's Betty doing? How do I explain this to my parents? They seem so removed from this sort of situation. Here come the University Police. They try to look official. Somewhat comical to see them come rushing in with stretcher and blankets. After all, I <u>can</u> walk. They try valiantly to amuse me. Somewhat pathetic display of concern. Still snowing. Not much colder. What happens now? I've tried <u>it</u>. Still depressed. I'm not very violent certainly. I suppose I'll live. Have I commanded attention? Who knows already? Who should be informed? Best to be hush-hush and mysterious. Doctor at Health Services keeps plaguing me all night (although can't sleep anyhow) for temperature and blood samples. Betty called. I'm to call the long-distance operator to speak with her. (It seems that there actually <u>was</u> some activity precipitated by more action.) (They went to my dorm and checked all the windows, searched all over for a body. God, <u>they</u> must have been more worried than I. Operators tracing calls. Proctors called. An Assistant Dean alerted. Such attention.

Gratifying or does it now seem somewhat ridiculous?) Betty is very openly disturbed. How could I do it? (No answer.) Remember that she loves me? (Had I forgotten or did I need proof? <u>We all need proof.</u>) Nurse says I must stop talking on phone. Private room (this must be to isolate me from others). Must I leave the University? Must my parents know? I'm still depressed, and now somewhat humiliated. (Maybe humiliation is what I needed.) I never slept that night. Got considerably worse in health (that ringing in my ears seemed persistent.) I was told that parents must be notified. Either I or University official must call. If I call then they can determine from my voice that I'm still on earth. It seems difficult, but I tell them "I tried to take my life (<u>the one they gave me,</u> is that unfair?). Don't worry I'm still alive. You don't need to come (what a futile suggestion of mine). Why don't you talk to the doctor? he knows what it's all about." I was kept for a week of observation, testing, discussion. Those damn questions seemed so specific. How can I answer them with any certainty? There is no certainty. And yet I thought there was at least the certainty of death. If things (life) were only so easily containable, as I had thought last Saturday. Now I'll be on referral for the rest of the year. Wonder what psychiatrists are like (couch? Jewish? pad and pencil? ask lots of question? potted plants?. . .)? Apparently I'm not going to die. Death could <u>never</u> be so apparent.

My emotions were, as I hope this reconstruction of the sequence demonstrates, fluctuating considerable in the course of the evening. I don't think I really wanted to die; I did want attention; circumstances (isolation, paper, failure to communicate with the two girls, weather, darkness, need for some commotion) did conspire; suicide seemed logical, reasonable, remarkably calm. I would interpret my attempt as a "Cry for Help." My self-estimation and confidence were so deficient as to warrant the analysis depressed. And yet, I still cannot conceive of my action as violent, or wrong. It was the moment at which I was most susceptible to my own negative suggestion. I had always characterized myself as one of the morbid types, constantly self-incriminating. It was as much an attempt to satisfy my own conception of myself as depressed, as it was the act of depression. At the moment when I realized that death was not assured (despite the fact that I was later told that the dosage had been lethal and only time was required) I began to wonder what others would think, I began to feel some embarrassment, and I began to wonder about objective things (Could I have an extension on the paper? I must be able to study in the Infirmary. What are a psychiatrist's fees? What explanations could be afforded my roommates for my absence?etc.) And yet I was for a moment intensely serious about the potential death offered as an option on life. It is challenging to consider this action, in retrospect, a self-evident appeal for attention; that seems, however, to have been the particular case. As in the case of the Steppenwolf, I have come to recognize that attention and concern may be prejudiced by me and that I may obscure the efforts of others to know me through too great an effort to know myself without the social context of relationships and interaction. I have since found a more satisfying sexual relationship; this circumstance has contributed significantly to a more positive self-reflection. I felt, as perhaps Hesse rediscovered in the course of Steppenwolf and The Journey to the East, that I cannot be my own "magic theatre," but must enjoy others and not prohibit them from enjoying me. The attempt described above seems to have been of long-range benefit, although I hesitate to call a suicidal attempt "beneficial" or "benevolent." Perhaps the attempt would have been avoided if the distinction between dying and death had been defined earlier. I must now subscribe to Hesse's encouraging suggestion in the Steppenwolf:

> "We demonstrate to anyone whose soul has fallen to pieces that he can rearrange these pieces of a previous self in what order he pleases, and so attain to an endless multiplicity of moves in the game of life. As the playwright shapes a drama from a handful of characters, so do we from the pieces of the disintegrated self build up ever new groups, with ever new interplay and suspense, and new situations that are eternally inexhaustible."
>
> (Hesse, Steppenwolf, p.217)

Chapter 13

Psychological Death and Resurrection

Anonymous

The four-year college experience frequently results in an inability to reach maturity. The phenomenon of "prolonged adolescence" has been amply documented; it is common in college students and is characterized by the avoidance of ego-conflict by means of narcissistic defenses. "Wherever he is (this adolescent) follows the scheme of infantile identity maintenance which says, 'I am what others believe me to be.'" (Peter Blos. On Adolescence. New York: Free Press, 1962. p. 224).

The difficult movement toward reality-based self-awareness, the growing acceptance of death, and the consequent conclusion that he too has a right to a life are not taught the late adolescent. These things are not discussed or learned at college, usually, but they may happen. Indeed they may happen whether the Self controls it or not, even though what he has experienced and how he has evaluated those experiences may provide the impetus.

It is not immediately obvious why any adolescent would enroll in a course on death and suicide in the dead of winter, especially since the age group 18-22 has a low lethality, if high perturbation, rating. Death has approached few lives of this length, and so one suspects that the student is inquiring not about death itself, but about a psychological state which he equates with death. That is, he may feel dead. He may feel loneliness and anxiety and depression beginning in the freshman year not alleviated even after graduation. That the course on death finally enrolled 150 college age people was, in February, a first perhaps healthy sign that some people had recognized the poverty of their existences.

The nature of events at Harvard this spring and the subsequent feelings of hostility and alienation--

always present but then finally brought out in the open-- demand that someone examine them, however superficially, in relation to the maturation process of the individual. The social demands of the strike were well-known. What was going on in the individuals is still far from clear, but is far more important.

This paper is an attempt to discuss, from a personal point of view, my own awareness of death suddenly this winter and to chart the developments from this awareness through the general strike at Harvard in April. The belief that individual emotional response to the environment was the cause of the strike, and not a concern with moral questions, and that the emotional turmoil was ultimately healthy are basic assumptions of the paper.

An autobiographical examination is always a difficult task, and here it is especially so since all the circumstances surrounding this case are unusual, if not extraordinary. The points that are made, however, are selected as being essential to the final mystical experience concerning death.

My parents were divorced when I was eight, thereby, one supposes, starting many conflicts in my young mind. The fact that my mother was anxious to find a new husband as quickly as possible was therefore frustrating enough to precipitate a severe onset of asthma when I was eleven. The disease continued to be troublesome for four years, in which time I was hospitalized at least once each year. During the ages 15-19 it was relatively quiet and flared up irregularly.

Having attended preparatory school and spending that summer after graduating withdrawing libido from an unrequiting love object -- another boy two years younger than myself -- I entered Harvard reluctant to begin all over again; I was anxious and uninterested in people. Thus the seeds were planted for the familiar schizophrenic behavior of adolescence. The environment encouraged, rather than remedied or even remained neutral about, this disturbance.

The first term was relatively quiet symptomatically, although I had a few weeks trouble in November. I developed a "working relationship" with my roommate. Since he hated "preppies" when he first got here, and I hated football players, we had our mutual prejudices to work on first. The January exams went well, and I realized that I enjoyed school enough to major in history.

During the fall asthma flare-up a doctor at the Health Services put me on a drug. After exams I proceeded to take myself off it abruptly, precipitating a severe attack. I was hospitalized and put back on the drug.

By March, however, I developed another and more serious symptom: severe pain in my left arm. I was admitted to the hospital infirmary and finally, by the end of the six-week incarceration, there was for the first time serious talk that I would need surgery, an amputation for a malignant tumor.

As complicated as this picture was, another even more so was being drawn on the interpersonal level. Another friendship took shape, but one in which the ambivalences were more obvious. After three months of attempting to integrate the relationship, we were not getting along well. Each wanted the other to substantiate Self, confirm Self, admire Self, while neither was able or willing to do this.

Unfortunately we had already committed ourselves to rooming together in the House with a third boy, who was a known homosexual. This third member had latched on to the other boy earlier in the term and the two had made some sort of rooming arrangement before I came on the scene. One can postulate now that my friend was eager to include me in the set-up to act as a buffer between him and the other fellow, who was threatening to him.

These medical and social problems had a subtle depersonalizing effect on me. In preparation for the surgery I was withdrawing a little from my body. I began to think of myself almost completely as a creature of thought, a poet.

These are the defenses of a sick person, and I used them in personal relationships as well. By the end of the term I was reasonably convinced that life was little more than a passive game, an endurance test, if you will, a constant bid for attention counteracted by resentment over being treated either as a patient or a tool. My inner world, on the other hand, continued to be imaginatively elaborate, and I wrote a great deal.

At any rate freshman year drew to a close. The surgery was set up in Boston. As far as the operation was concerned both parents, now remarried, were frightened and communicated this fright to me. There was also, of course, some relief that the disease would be arrested, for as my mother complained, "You just don't know what it's like to have a sick kid." She was, in her usual way, speaking to me.

Following the surgery I seemed to have little trauma over the body image. I used the defense of intellectualization: the routine of learning to use the prosthesis was imperative to learn, etc. The hate, the rage, the fear, and the grief didn't come to the surface until a suicide attempt at school that fall.

The setting was the previously mentioned rooming situation which had disintegrated by October into a state of hopeless mutual alienation and in fact hostility. I solved the problem by either getting drunk or going to the library, but these maneuvers, did not, of course, solve much at all. The other two similarly spent as much time as possible either physically or psychologically out of the small room.

The alienation was encouraged also by the impersonality of the House system, which manages to give one the impression that everyone else has something interesting and important to do. People tumble into the large cafeteria-dining hall three times a day in an almost ritualized fashion to eat with the faces they must at all costs remain friendly to. The most unforgivable evil is to dislike anyone. This is important because so many identities depend on being liked by everyone. Naturally the identity thus maintained isn't very complicated, or indeed very human, as ideally it must appear (and often is) conflict-free. Asocial behavior is, in a dormitory, unrewarding at best anyway.

Into the midst of the jangled rooming arrangements, the alcohol, the sophomore year, the prosthetic adjustments came a letter from my father wherein he called one of my roommates a "boyfriend, oh excuse me," and within the hour I had swallowed twelve seconals. I woke after nine hours in Cambridge Hospital, having been found by one of the roommates, which I am still not sure about.

On returning to Harvard and the university infirmary I was "rescued" (those were the days of adolescent rescue fantasy, where one searches for the <u>one thing</u> which will make life intelligible, controllable, and happy) from some dire alternatives by a Health Services psychiatrist, and it was decided I could stay in school under therapy. I was able to move out of my hellish rooming menage a trois almost immediately, and the next two years settled down to a more healthy mental outlook, even though I was still confronted with the schizogenic Harvard community.

Finally this January I was once again living in solitude, studying hard for exams and trying to write a thesis when a terrifying revelation crashed down on me. (But I am now assuming that after all the anesthetics, morphine, sleeping pills, and the suicide attempt that have characterized the last three years, this terror was a major breakthrough toward an integrated self.)

It began when a dining hall conversation on falling out of an airplane turned my imagination to the last seconds of the fall. What happened at the end of the fall? What was it like to die?

The idea began to obsess me. Nobody was willing to discuss it, there were evidently no books available on it. No one could even understand why I was worrying about it. Please drop it, I was told.

That, of course, frightened me all the more.

Finally one evening I was invited to smoke some marijuana with some casual acquaintances, and since I thought the pot might take my mind off death, I complied. What happened, however, was the opposite of my expectations: death suddenly seemed to be an immediate certainty, and I went over the brink into pure terror.

Happily my relationship with my psychiatrist is such that I could telephone him, and his assurances that such anxieties, or phobias, were common (which may or may not be accurate) helped to dispell some of the fear and loneliness.

The following weeks were quieter. I read philosophy and poetry, and continued to write my thesis. I stayed away from people however because I could no longer bear the superficial quality of all the conversations to be had, vague and listless as they were. And of course the subject preoccupying me was not an acceptable topic for conversation anyway.

It seems now to have been inevitable that given my romantic bent all of this would have led to a mystical experience, so-called. What the mind is and what the ego's conscious and unconscious relationship to the other functions of the mind is not clear to me at least, so I am reluctant to smile knowingly and say that I received emanations from somewhere beyond myself. What happened was certainly the product of mental areas which the limited consciousness called self had barely noticed before, much less experienced.

At the time I was schizophrenically and fearfully depersonalized. The confusion about what self was was so great that I could not look in a mirror without feeling that what I saw was an entirely separate entity from "I," which I began to believe to be purely spiritual.

Two new personal relationships were encouraging such thinking. The first new friend, attracted in the dining hall, was an alcoholic and very suicidal -- (he talked about his suicide fantasy with zeal) -- a senior, who felt that I was the only person in the world whom he could "talk to." The other was another senior, but an only child who tried to maintain that status while at Harvard and was consequently very lonely and hung up on his identification with his mother, one imagines. Be that as it may, he also thought I was a good person to sit and watch television with -- no need for conversation, we have an understanding -- while I was quite plainly trying to get the thesis written.

I, the object, began to take walks. I tried desperately to focus my attention on something beyond me in the real world. The more I looked at the people around me, the more it seemed that they were just rubbery dolls with no personalities, no inner vitality or strength; just a body which they drove around in to go to classes, eat, sleep, make small talk. It was horrifying.

I had by this time almost completely separated what I called me from the everyday world, feeling that it, and my body, were responsible for my mortality. The horror of this depersonalization lasted for weeks. I was certain I was mad.

The thesis done, I moved into another room with two other seniors unknown to me (the mechanics of the rooming situations for this year are complex and probably irrelevant), and I began to apply a little reason to the problem. I began to realize that first of all I had been living two lives. One self had been for the outside world, the doctors, and peers; and the other had been self as experienced by me. I had been encouraged to pay more attention to the objective self, and had started to feel that all there was to me was what other people saw. In other words, the environment had urged me to commit a kind of psychological suicide. With the terror of that pot-revealing evening I was even consciously trying to destroy the ego so that I would not feel death when it struck. Yes, definitely weird.

But at this time I was using a little reason. The academic pressures were lifted when the thesis was finished at the beginning of March, and I decided the time had come to tell those who were treating me as an object to go straight to hell, which I did, and which they did not do until much later. I saw the schizophrenic nature of the past few years, and was able to read enough to make that label meaningful to me. Life continued to be, however, a rather passive routine, even with all these exciting insights. A few people assured me that "the vision will fade, as visions do." But such was not to be.

One evening I was falling asleep in my new, isolated but not lonely room; I began to dream of an electric lamp, focusing my attention on its cord as much as on the lamp itself. With part of my mind I could feel that rolling tide of sensation which had awakened me many nights over the past months. I still cannot account for it; it felt, physically, like a yawn inside my head. It had kept me up annoyingly before because it gave me some anxiety and I had always woke myself before it reached its conclusion, whatever it was. This was not the sensation, familiar to us all, of falling and catching ourselves, or having a relaxing muscle twitch, as we drift off to sleep.

The dream this time kept me asleep, more or less, until it was over: the sensation culminated in a violent electric _shock._ It clobbered me for a few seconds and left my mind, my brain, feeling very "full" and warm and glowing. Let me apologize for the poetic description. I still cannot account for what happened. My leg twitched during the onslaught and I am wondering whether it wasn't some kind of brain wave synchronization found in epilepsy. Whatever it was, it was not a dream, and it was not in the beginning familiar to me; I had been fighting it for months. Then it was over and I eventually fell asleep.

The next day I woke to notice how incredibly drab and empty my room was. I dashed out to find posters, mobiles, flowers, expenses I am still paying for, anything and everything that was colorful, interesting, stimulating. I felt how emotionally and intellectually starved I was for experience from the outside world. The fantasy world of my imagination could no longer hold the fort.

So much happened physically, emotionally, and spiritually during the next few weeks that it is difficult to tell everything.

I continued to take walks and had insomnia. As I walked day and night, stalking the Yard and the streets to the north, I felt like some huge, walking penis. Indeed one of the first things I noticed was a tremendous increase of sensitivity there. I felt physical. I felt alive. I felt _here_, not hidden somewhere in the depths of my body.

The whole trip was permeated by Kierkegaard's "uncanniness." I did begin to not merely believe in God, but slowly began to feel more and more insignificant before Him. There seemed to be a real texture to the universe that I had never noticed before.

But this was not a bed of roses. Feeling like an exposed penis gave me a lot of castration anxiety which later turned into fantasies of being killed. Because I did feel so open to attack, I began to hate the environment; the heavy buildings, the multitudes of cars, the noise, the bustle. It seemed so ridiculously unimportant in the face of the weird, and yet it didn't budge. It resisted any effort made to become a feeling human being. And so, I began to hate it.

All the hostility I had ever felt and suppressed, or turned against myself,seemed to roar out into Cambridge, destroying. I felt, in my fear, all-powerful, completely omnipotent. I frequently, indeed almost constantly, fantasized the end of the world. This too of course is a schizophrenic characteristic.

Where before I had severely differentiated myself from the real world, effecting depersonalization, now I was uncertain where reality began and my mind stopped. Everything was a crazy mishmash of emotion which screamed only, "I am alive. Let me be alive!"

The body image problem slowly resolved itself. Physically at least, I saw where I left off and where I existed in reality. I finally was noticing the effects of the surgery, which had turned me from a chronically ill person into a vigorous, healthy (although crippled) human being. Health, absent all these years, was so exhilarating that it gave me the sensation of absolute power.

And the hate, fear, and disgust I felt for the environment was not easily dispelled. And the emotion, while incapable of destroying the world, did affect other people; in fact the emotional balance of a competitive and closed community such as this seemed especially vulnerable to the psychotic and directed rage of one person. But it must be realized that the hate and anger were not at first controlled. I did not decide to feel that way; those emotions were a defensive response to what I felt to be a singularly hostile world. The very passivity and unconcern of other people was <u>hostile</u> to me at the time.

Weeks later, during the general university strike at Harvard, people said to me, as this one did, "You know, the anonymity of the first few years here was fun. But now, it isn't fun anymore."

The Strike, from this point of view then, was a violent endeavor to establish personal integrity by a large number of individuals, an attempt to integrate Self in a society which ignores the self in favor of the grey murky mass. Because no one was quite sure what was going on in that Strike (as we heard many people disclose with a great deal of anxiety in their voices) and because people assumed that it was primarily an awakening <u>social</u> consciousness at work, they attended mass meetings and rallies and discussions with hoards of others. In fact, however, they might have done much better to have simply looked at themselves, the real source of the turmoil. Harvard, as a potentially stimulating and dynamic community, needed to become aware of these tiny islands of confusion. The fears of adolescence and prolonged-adolescence -- over sexual identity, grades, self-image, social success, what to do with all this time! -- seemingly have crippled this college. All of us have felt the depersonalization, the unconcern that is fundamental to even the "closest" friendships, or boy-girl romances. At the time of the Strike we all felt it at one time, and hence the chaos.

It is a consequence of living in a small community of introspective people who for defensive reasons -- there are too many (?) of us crammed together in the same place trying to live identical roles -- treat each other as objects, that sameness take the place of surprise and interest. Getting drunk, smoking pot, sleeping, masturbating, studying, take the place of hard interpersonal contact with objective reality. The longer we treat each other as object, thus killing the arrogant potentials and curiosities of the human being, the more certain it becomes that we will <u>become</u> objects, schizophrenic, walking corpses, to coin a phrase.

The role that the awareness of "death," an abstraction which covers almost too much territory, played in integration was and is crucial. Since death is not an experience, and yet happens; since we are sure that there is no God, and yet are not so sure in private, judging from the results of the questionnaire; since we just "don't know" about immortality, the difficulties of coping with physical death are bad enough. We must also deal with psychological death, the temptation is great to forget about the whole topic, as many who attended the first Soc Rel 155 lecture did, saying it was far too "morbid" for a winter afternoon. But ironically, one must die emotionally or "spiritually" in order to cope with death in this way. That alternative looks easier, but most of us who have taken the opportunity to develop <u>something</u> in the past months and become a bit more self-aware, would shudder at that oblivion as more horrible than the certain oblivion of physical death. Of course there is pain and fear in maturing and integrating. But if all the literature

I have been exposed to and if all the people I have superficially encountered have taught me anything, it is that it is better to have lived and lost than never to have lost at all.

PART V

THOUGHTS ON CONTEMPORARY PHILOSOPHERS

Chapter 14

Death in the Philosophy of Jean-Paul Sartre

Richard Ruiz

The problem of death has always haunted man--precisely because its true nature is unknowable. Man is instinctively a metaphysician, and thus his whole history is concerned with the problems caused by the unknowable. It is of prime importance to note that all the philosophies that have ever been created as an ethic for life have been determined by a certain conception of what lies beyond the grave. It has been said that God created man because he was bored with his eternal, all-knowing existence; God has created no philosophies, since for him there are no unknowables. It is man who must learn to live in the face of the ultimate mystery of death, and thus it is he who has invented multiple religions to help him explain his life in relation to that mystery.

Existentialism is of this stuff, since it is a commentary on life. We will see how it has contributed much to the study of death in direct relation to man. I have focused on Sartre because of his peculiar way of treating the subject of death. For him, death as well as life are a total absurdity: he gives us no reassuring _raison d'etre_. It is this absolute hopelessness which he has in the future--and therefore in the present--which makes us view him as a veritable "philosopher of despair."

By way of introduction, one should note initially the contribution which existentialism in general has made to the study of death. One can start by making a simple but not-so-insignificant distinction: that between death as an _act_, and death as a _state_ or condition. Traditionally, no distinction--no qualitative distinction, at least-of this genre had been made; the act of death was seen merely as the first act of the state of death. The act of death was therefore classed as a "non-life" act. The Christian view of death seems to fit this description: death here is something entirely non-human, the beginning of "something better", the gate to eternal life. Epicurus expressed much the same idea when he said that death was "the moment of life which I never have to live..."

Existentialists have taken death out of its non-life context and have placed it, at least in one sense, on the same scale with birth and the other major _human_ events. Sartre (1956, p.531) explains this position in the introduction to his section in _Being and Nothingness_ called "My Death":

> After death had appeared to us as pre-eminently non-human, since it was what was on the other side of the "wall", we decided suddenly to consider it from a wholly different point of view--that is, as an event of human life.

The phenomenon of death became something which is on "this side" of the wall; no longer was it the first act in the state of death. Rather, it became the last term in a series of life-acts. As Sartre eloquently points out in typical paradoxical fashion, death is the limit of life, but because it is also a part of life, "Life is limited by life". This view of death is also a commentary on the unique nature of man and his relation to death. On the one hand, he exists--but in that, he is no different from other existents; he is unique in that he knows that he exists, but more than that, he can anticipate the future: he knows he is going to die. James Diggory (1967, p.307) says it better than I can: "Man's uniqueness _qua_ man is conditioned on the knowledge that he is going to die." In this way, a man's death is always a part of his life: he exists only in the face of death, only in the knowledge that his existence is limited.

There is another aspect of death which existentialists have helped clear up for us; this is illustrated by the distinction they make between "death" and "my death." Death as a universal phenomenon is interesting in itself, but it does not come to the point exactly. Kierkegaard, "the first existentialist", pointed out that he who knows that "all men are mortal" knows an abstract, theoretical truth about man in general, but what really counts is that "I, too, must die". Max Stirner, the young German Hegelian of the nineteenth century, made this same point when he said that "'man' is but a fiction, a ghost,...only the individual is real" (Choron, 1963, p.223).

To speak of "man" or of "humanity" is not of ultimate importance to the existentialist; nor is he concerned so much with the general concept of death. He would rather speak of "my death" (since that will show itself to be my only real concern) and of my way of facing death now. He is not interested in thinking of death as the cessation of heartbeat or respiration: such things are all irrelevant to me; I will not be observing or evaluating my death; I will have to do it.

Death, therefore, is not so important as a general phenomenon which all experience; its significance lies in that it is a deeply personal, life-event which each must face. But there is another point which existentialism has made clearer for us: it has drawn our attention even more than ever before to the fact that death is an experience which can and does come at any moment. Here, it has merely taken the cue from the Christian doctrine that one never knows when death will strike, and that therefore one should be always ready for it. This is diametrically opposed to another idea, sometimes called the naturalistic view of death, which sees death as the last in a series of very predictable steps in the development (birth-childhood-adolescence-adulthood-oldage-death) of the life cycle. This view is expounded by Max Scheler in the following passage from Jolivet (1950, p.31):

> La mort...se presente a nous comme une limite que l'on peut prevoir en observant le developpement du processus que constitue le vieillissement: a chaque minute de ma vie, le passe accroit sa pression et les possibilites de l'avenir se retrecissent de plus en plus; ma liberte, conditionee par l'exuberance de la vie, perd chaque jour de son ampleur, jusqu'au jour ou la vieillesse m'en depouillera a pue pres completement. La mort n'est que l'achevement de ce processus de destruction continue et je l'eprouve approchante et comme deja presente dans cette ruine progressive et inexorable de mon etre.

The shallowness of Scheler's thought here can be easily seen. His description seems to concern itself more with the process of aging (vieillissement) than with the event of death. If all deaths were merely a product of old age, then they would indeed be predictable, but even then only to a point. But death almost never arrives at the "appropriate" time. It is not always the natural consummation of the life cycle; as Sartre (1956, p.533) himself says, every attempt to consider death "as a resolved chord at the end of a melody must be sternly rejected". This would merely be overlooking such common facts as senility and premature death, and at the same time subordinating man's awareness of his own death. We will see later how Sartre uses this idea of the unpredictable arrival of death to show its effects on the meaning man gives to life.

Existential thinkers, then, have performed a service in calling our attention to the phenomenology of personal death. They have noted that death is important as a basis for philosophy not because it is universal and inevitable, but because it is personal and entirely unpredictable. My death is not universal, it is _mine_; I am not replaceable in dying my death, _I_ have to die it; I know that I am going to die, but I don't know _when._ (The importance of _why_ and _how_ I die does not seem to enter the discussion).

But there is a problem in this concept of experiencing one's own death which must be cleared up in relation to the existentialists. Heidegger, probably the most prominent existentialist, tries to cope with the problem: "Death does not reveal itself as a loss, but rather as a loss experienced by the survivors..We do not experience in a genuine sense the dying of others but are at most 'present'" (Kaufman, 1959, p.46). The implication here is that it is in fact impossible to experience one's own death. That is the same thought which Sartre (1956, p.535) expresses in the following passage:

> ...there is no personalizing virtue which is peculiar to _my_ death. Quite the contrary, it becomes my death only if I place myself already in the perspective of subjectivity.

Again, he states the idea: "It is my subjectivity that makes my death _my_ death". Man is at once aware of the presence of others and he is more certain of this than of himself. In that same way, he does experience the death of others while he can only anticipate his own.

How, then, to reconcile this idea with the previous one, the one which states that only I can experience my own death? The problem arises because we are speaking of death as two different things. On the one hand, death is a general idea the results of which we feel deeply; on the other, death is an experience in which we participate insofar as is possible (i.e. up to the cessation of consciousness). In that sense, not the results of death, but the awareness of and preparation for my death are the important factors. Insofar as anyone can experience the event of death (not the results of it), only I can experience my death.

By way of summing up this section of the paper: Existentialism has made some important contributions to our view of death; first, it has emphasized that it is very much a part of life of which man is always aware; second, it accentuates the personal nature of death as an event which, insofar as it can be experienced, can be experienced only by me; third, it shows that death can come at any time. Sartre agrees with these general existentialist ideas; it is my task now to show the peculiarities in Sartre's concept of death.

Initially, I will have to submit a very unsatisfactory definition of death as Sartre sees it. He himself never gives a cogent and all-embracing definition; his notion of death must be extracted from the whole of his work. But, in order to establish a base from which to work, let me cite these two descriptions of death--descriptions which seem to come closest to the sartrean definition of death.

1. "That which reveals itself as indiscoverable, that which disarms all expectations."
2. "Death haunts me at the cove of each of my projects as their inavoidable obverse." (Choron,1963,p.247).

After descriptions like these, all one gets are terse and not-too-telling phrases such as "mystere et source d'angoisse", "aneantissement de l'etre", "ecroulement final de la vie". By examining some of his ideas on man and existence, we may gain some insight into his notion of "nothingness".

In Sartre, there is an underlying assumption that our minds can comprehend something only by contrasting it with its negation (Wild,1955,p.119); this is best demonstrated in the realm of feeling: one better understands health (and better appreciates it) when one experiences sickness; one sees freedom in a different light as an ex-slave, and so on. This also holds true for the concept of being. The study of nothingness in Sartre is not an idle study; it is from its examination that we extract any meaning to "being" in the sartrean system.

Nothingness for Sartre has its source in man himself. He concludes this from his idea of the two fundamental kinds of being--Being-In-Itself (_en soi_)and Being-For-Itself (_pour soi_). Being-In-Itself is defined as "non-conscious being"; it is everything that is. Being-For-Itself is conscious being, being which is free in its existence, and therefore responsible for it. Since everything "that is" exists _en soi_, we find that _pour soi_ must be everything that "is not"--nothingness. Where does nothingness come from? By definition, it is everything that is not _en soi_, and so cannot find its origin there. If we look at man, we see that the _pour soi_ applies only to him; it is only he who is free to choose his existence. But man (his body, at any rate) is also _en soi_. It follows, then, that nothingness comes from that element in man which makes him more than just a body, which makes him human--the _pour soi_, his freedom. Since the _en soi_ does not have to understand things by comparing them with their negation, since indeed the _en soi_ is incapable of comprehending anything, a distinction between being and nothingness is irrelevant _to it._ It is only in man that this distinction becomes important; it is in man therefore that one finds the origin of nothingness.

It is all-important to see how the significance man ascribes to nothingness (that which makes him unique in existence) affects his being. Man, of course, is what he is and what he has been; but for existentialists, he is even more than that: he is the future that he projects ahead of himself. Existential philosophers before Sartre, primarily Heidegger, have concluded from this idea that death is necessary for the completeness of the individual. Because man is the future that he projects ahead of himself, and because this future exists only as possibility, man is incomplete: human wholeness demands the limit of death. Only at death is the true evaluation of a man's life possible; only then is the structure of his real possibilities revealed. (Manser,1966, p.66):

> At the moment of death, we <u>are</u>, that is to say we are without defense against the judgment of others; it can be decided what we really were, we have no chance of escaping from a summing up such as an all-knowing intelligence might make.

This is Heidegger's main premise in asserting that man is more than anything a "Being-Toward-Death": "L'homme est fondamentalement un etre-pour-la-mort et il n'y a de liberte que pour assumer la mort" (Jolivet, 1950,p.13). He is saying, essentially, that only death--the external limit of man's life--can give life its meaning. He almost utters the Christian doctrine that one should be always prepared for death; more, that the very purpose of life is a waiting and a preparation for death.

Sartre condemns the whole idea of death as an absurdity; this is in part a result of what he thinks death is. Sartre (1956,p.540) cites Malraux in what now has become an almost familiar aphorism: "Death converts life into destiny." He continues to say that, with my death, the <u>other</u> takes care of my life; he means by this that each of us must continually remind himself that he is the subject of a future alienation by which we belong to the other as soon as we die. Death thus becomes a complete negation and annulment of life where there is no future, no subjective freedom, and no conscious mobility.

But death is also an absurdity because of its relationship with the For-Itself. The For-Itself is perpetual desire, while death is the end of all desire. When death appears, the For-Itself disappears; as soon as I die, I disappear into the In-Itself. There, the dead life will undergo changes without being responsible for them. Nothing happens to it from the "inside"; it is completely closed and nothing can enter into it. The nature of the In-Itself is exteriority: it is not a subjective world, and consequently it is not a world in which the For-Itself could survive.

There is, therefore, no place for death in the For-Itself. That seems to be the ultimate in absurdity. Man, after all, is the only existent that is consciously affected by the concept of death; he is the only one capable of understanding and anticipating nothingness. Thus, nothingness is only relevant when discussing man. Yet, in the essence of man, the For-

Itself, there is no place for death.

There is more in this concept of the For-Itself. I have mentioned before that man is what he is, what he has been, and what he projects himself to be; futurity, then, becomes of prime importance. The For-Itself is a being which always demands a future, and it is for that reason that there is no place for death there. Life cannot be a preparation for death; it cannot be an event which renders meaning to life; it cannot be waited for. Waiting for death merely destroys itself, for death is the negation of all waiting. Death is an absurd possibility, for it is a possibility which ends as possibilities.

The mere fact that death is an inevitability is not enough, however, to render it totally absurd. What characterizes the absurd quality of death to a greater degree is its arbitrary nature and inopportune arrival. One cannot wait for death, because its arrival time is never known for sure: "If only deaths from old age existed (or deaths by explicit condemnation), then I could wait for my death" (Sartre,1956, p.535). But, because one is subject to the arbitrary whim of the "other", the time of my death can never be determined. Death is not rooted in our freedom, and because of that, Sartre will disagree with Heidegger: if we cannot choose the time of our death, then the meaning of life escapes us. If "what we are" (which is determined at the moment of death) is very dependent on the very minute of death, then our life has no meaning unless we can choose the time to end it. I can use no better anecdote to illustrate this than the one Sartre (1956, p.538) borrowed from Diderot:

> Two brothers appeared at the divine tribunal on the Day of Judgment. The first said to God, "Why did you make me die so young?" And God said, "In order to save you. If you had lived longer, you would have committed a crime as your brother did". Then the brother in turn asked, "Why did you make me die so old?" If death is not the free determination of our being, it cannot complete our life. If one minute more or less may perhaps change everything and if this minute is added to or removed from my account, then even admitting that I am free to use my life, the meaning of life escapes me.

The last point I will mention here may be a good conclusion to a discussion of Sartre's views on death. Nothingness, the negation of life, is a very important element in life; its importance is accentuated, however, by the fact that man is aware of this future nothingness, that he anticipates it, and in some cases even prepares for it. Death, then, is not the real phenomenon to which Sartre will give uppermost significance; rather, it is man's awareness of his own finitude. That all men die is not important; what is important is that all men are mortal. That, after all, is the basis of all philosophies--a justification of life and a social ethic which is based on a certain conception of the state of death. But Sartre seems to revolt against that kind of philosophizing: he creates an ethic which pretends to be totally oblivious to its own conception of death. Put more correctly, while most philosophies are created because of a certain view of death, Sartre creates his little branch of existentialism _in spite of_ his view of death. He fails at his task, for all he can say to his fledgeling existentialist man is that life and death are unexplainable absurdities--an unconvincing argument, and almost a cop-out.

But maybe that is not the point at all. The point may be that the whole of existentialism has missed the boat. It wants us to assume that death be accepted _phenomenologically_ as a "passage into nothingness". (Wild, 1955,p.219). It is unclear, however, that that can be the logically conclusion from an observation of phenomenon. All we observe is a cessation of animation; whether what animates the body persists or vanishes into nothingness is not observed.

Howbeit, Sartre has some logic in his premises. But in the end he is not prepared to say more than that death is the "end". If we accept this, what lies after death is of importance only to the academic. Sartrean existentialism offers us no assurance for the future, or even for the present. If we accept his ideology, we must resign ourselves to an absurd and meaningless life; if we are too sensitive for such a life, we will turn elsewhere to a more sympathetic religion. The choice is ours: each, after all, is ultimately responsible for his own philosophy.

References

Choron,Jacques. _Death and Western Thought._ New York:

Collier, 1963.

Choron,Jacques. Death as a Motive of Philosophic Thought. In E.S. Shneidman (Ed.), Essays in Self-Destruction. New York: Science House, 1967.

Desan, Wilfrid. The Tragic Finale. Cambridge: Harvard University Press, 1954.

Diggory, James C. The Components of Personal Despair. In E.S. Shneidman (Ed.), Essays in Self-Destruction. New York: Science House, 1967.

Jolivet, Regis. Le Probleme de la mort. Paris: Editions de Fontenelle, 1950.

Kaufmann, Walter. Existentialism and Death. In Herman Feifel (Ed.), The Meaning of Death, New York: McGraw-Hill, 1959.

Manser, Anthony. Sartre: A Philosophic Study. University of London: The Athlone Press, 1966.

Pascal, Blaise. Pensees. New York: E.P. Dutton & Company, 1958.

Sartre, Jean-Paul. Being and Nothingness. (Translated by H.E. Barnes) New York: Philosophic Library,1956.

Wild, John. The Challenge of Existentialism. Bloomington: Indiana University Press, 1955.

Chapter 15

Unamuno and Death

Gregory W. Hornig

Philosophers have forever been obsessed with the significance of death and many of their beliefs have been structured on the basis of man's possible extinction. Unamuno (1950,p.11) shows this same concern, and he says:

> "El unico verdadero problema vital, del que mas a las entranas nos llega, del problema de nuestro destino individual y personal, de la immortalidad del alma.." (Rough translation: "The only vital problem that arises from our insides, which will determine our personal and individual destiny, is the question of the immortality of our souls.")

Miguel de Unamuno's main preoccupation, then, was the essence of man: his social condition on the one hand, and man's aspirations for immortality on the other, and finally, his susceptibility to death.

The irreconcilability of death is reflected in Unamuno's writing style. His inability to omit death from his thoughts creates difficult intellectual tensions, and leads Unamuno into agonizing introspection, giving all his works an axiological ambiguity of paradox and contradiction. What is shown in the following quotation is of relevance in several ways: it shows Unamuno's failure to become accommodated to a single desired truth, his failure to harmonize the marginal components of a single idea, and his penchant for adopting simultaneously two or three points of view. His writing style is significant in that it reflects his attitude to death: that of fear. Death, then, is the source of all his intellectual inspiration. Death is the only certainty, and this certainty must be destroyed only by creating a theory full of inner fragmentation, a theory that avoids the rational (death) and seeks the irrational (salvation). Unamuno

(1950,p.34) says, with all the torturous intellectual inner searchings of all existential thought:

> "Y si no muero, que sera de mi?; y si muero, ya nada tiene sentido. Y hav tres soluciones: a) o si que me muero del todo y entonces la desesperacion irremediable, o b) se que me muero del todo, y entonces la resignacion, o c) no puedo saber ni una ni otra cosa, y entonces la resignacion en la desesperacion o esta en aquella, una desperacion resignada, y LA LUCHA." And if I don't die, what

will become of me; and if I do die, then nothing has any feeling. And there are three solutions: a) that I die forever, and then irremediable desperation, or b) that I do not die and feel resigned to this fate, or c) that I cannot know either of these two possibilities, and feel resignation in desperation, or vice versa, a desperation in resignation, and suffer THE STRUGGLE.)

The last possibility is the one Unamuno elects. He cannot decide upon one rational choice, and turns to severe, and unfruitful introspection.

Unamuno is shrewd enough to perceive the danger of pure intellect. The only safeguard against the pure pursuit of intellectual logic is an irrationalist approach to all forms of valuation, including that of death. Since there is no unequivocal idea and since there is no single answer to an issue, Unamuno must entertain opposing and even contradictory statements with every issue. Unamuno forces the intellectual complexities of life upon himself and upon his writing. If he did the opposite, if he could successfully synthesize or reconcile opposite, he would come that much closer to the acceptance of death, the acceptance of death's finality to everything. The development of this thought proceeds as follows:

A. The lives of all individuals are characterized by the emnity of opposing factions within the ego. We are, in Unamuno's words, "the children of contradiction", the common matrix of dissident elements within a single organic body. This state of discord is itself a prime requisite to life. Why?

B. Because self-definition (and the escape of total death) is achieved through this state of discord.

For Unamuno, the right to behave inconsistently is the most fundamental human prerogative. Why? Because man's greatest goal is his integration with himself, the harmonization of his various selves (1950,p.44) ("The real one known only to God, the one each thinks himself to be, the ideal one each imagines the other to be..."), and this results only when there is agitation between these various selves. The problem of coordinating the differences of the "selves" is the existentialist dilemma, and only by suffering the existentialist dilemma can man harmonize the warring factions of his personality and begin to embark upon a profound spiritual experience, begin to assimilate his eternal Creator, and reject total death. How does Unamuno avoid death, then? The answer to this question is speculative because Unamuno offers so few straight answers. He thrives on paradox, and only when the Unamuno reader accepts paradox as his only cohesive device in assembling disharmonious elements can that reader begin to recognize identifiable forms and answers. Unamuno states at one point: "The greatest and most intimate of the many selves that each one of us bears is the self that each one wants to be, the self of our ambition." (Ilie,1967, p.114). And here lies the first paradox, and the first answer to Unamuno's struggle against his fear of total death.

The self which Unamuno designates the "greatest and most intimate" is also the most fictitious and the least real. Why is this? We must first understand that man's existence resides in his identification of the various selves which reveal themselves at different times in his life. Existence is but an acquisition and expenditure of selves, with one self remaining dominant, and performing the function of relegating the other selves--once dead--to memory. The life process continues and can be terminated only at the complete cessation of consciousness at death. What then is the significance of the "self of ambition?" Unamuno once said: "The person that I am today, my self today, buries my self of yesterday, just as my self of tomorrow will bury today's self.." (1959,Vol. VII,p.827). This partially explains his theory of the evolving selves, but seems to deny the normal concept of existence: the vital and continuous life. It does not, because Unamuno regarded only one thing as constant: the wish. His theory of existence is structured by an aggregation of fragmentary selves always evolving in the direction of destruction. The true self cannot be known if it is always evolving. The true self, then, is unimportant to Unamuno. Ingenious: (1959,Vol.IV, p.111) In lies La Vida de Don Quijote y Sanche: "What you are should be of little matter to you; uppermost for you is what you want to be. The being that you are is nothing but a decaying and fleeting being...the one that you want to be is your idea in God, the Consciousness of the Universe..."

This, then, is Unamuno's most clever refutation of eternal death. Man has existence, yet he continues to become. Once he is, then he dies, and is no longer. But by means of the wish (the "faith in faith itself" which will be discussed later), he can transcend his present condition of existential inconsistency, merge with the infinite, and defeat death. The attainment of integration comes from the necessary condition of existential inconsistency, therefore, and the imperative to "become" is possible through something which does not exist as yet: the realization of the wish. Death the Certainty can be defeated only through the Wish, the greatest of all Uncertainties.

Unamuno will not abandon his obsession for paradox. His very intellectual existence depends upon the incorporation of paradox into every thought, for paradox never allows the placid existence of a single and rational thought. At its basis is an irrational, dichotomous idea. And eternity--Unamuno's goal-- is irrational. So Unamuno's advice, though tortured with paradox and antithesis, is at least consistent. He says (1959, Vol. IX, p.732): "...allow them to seek you but not to find you, because the day they find you, you will no longer be you. Always be a hope; in other words, always be an enlightment (desengano), for on the day you are a memory, you will be a deception."

This is sage advice. The things that are most fully known--which have no aura of mystery, no mystic allurement, no apparent contradiction--are the things we are most apt to forget. Once forgotten, they are subjectively destroyed and left without real existence. The hope of salvation can therefore have the appearance of real vitality. The purely rational view of life can lack substance and vitality altogether, because it promises nothing but death. Along these lines Unamuno (1950) says: "La consecuencia vital del rationalismo sera el suicidio. Lo dice muy bien Kierkegaard: 'El suicidio es la consecuencia de existencia del pensamiento puro. 'No elegiamos el suicidio..." (The vital consequence of pure rationalism would be suicide. Kierkegaard says it very well: 'Suicide is the consequence of pure thought.' Let us not elect suicide...")

Pure rationalism could easily accept the reality of death and make existence only the expression of a void..Faith, (hope) the most irrational of all human sentiments can thwart the compulsive nearness of death. Without faith, we have the one alternative of suicide, according to Unamuno. Suicide would be the only answer to the monstrous folly of existence; to kill this monstrous falsification of reality, man would compulsively elect suicide.

Unamuno and Heidigger have similar outlines of existentialism in one aspect: the fear of death reveals the most authentic feature of existence. Unamuno, Kierkegaard, Sartre, Nietzsche and Rilke were all obsessed by the concept of death and its disturbing proximity to human life. We should now enter into a discussion of how their theories (Unamuno's in particular) differ with classical thought, and what solutions they offer to man's existential dilemma. Jacques Choron (1963,p.22) says that: "Existentialism is not concerned with man in general, but in his concrete individuality." The particular thinking of the existentialist philosophers, regardless of their otherwise very considerable differences," is described by Choron (p.223) as the "awareness of the fragility of Being..the terrifying possibility of non-being, and the horror of being."

Unamuno combats the fear of death by allowing his individual self to explore its own structure, its feelings, and its position with regard to everything that is not itself. The quest of consciousness, then, is the beginning of the Crusade against death. Only by confronting the empty core of reality can and must Unamuno affirm his own selfhood and declare a meaningful existence. Another paradox? No, because it is not in defiance to the self-contemplative state. Every individual knows that his level of abstraction can only be extended to cover a very limited span of Total Consciousness. To live without the slightest exercise of self-contemplation would be to exist in a relatively brute animal state, i.e., possessing individuality but not "persona." Human existence rises above the animal level in Nature when it has experienced the drama of self-awareness. So self-awareness is essential to man if he is to escape the cyclical destruction and reconstruction of the physical universe. Unamuno here enters into a worthwhile paradox, for while we avoid death by our self-consciousness of something supra-natural (the soul) we have also created death by our self-consciousness.

A note of caution, however. There is no causal connection between the act of cogitating non-existence and the fact of non-existence. But has it not been implied that death (non-existence)promotes consciousness of the "fragile self" and gives rise to various forms of existential anxiety? Yes, the speculation about death does indeed promote these flights of introspection, but the state of non-existence promotes no further human consciousness because death is a finality, wherein consciousness is terminated.

This gives rise to another thought mentioned by Choron: the refutation of Cartesian rationalization of existence, the existentialist refutation of "cogito ergo sum." Choron (1963,p.224) says "The secular heirs of Kierkegaard, however, little concerned with sin, took over his revolt against intellectualistic essentialism of post-Cartesian thought and his discovery of despair and dread as a means of apprehending reality..."

Descartes statement of "cogito ergo sum" is pure rationality, for thinking (cogito) is identical to being (sum), and schematically, cogito equals sum. Unamuno cannot accept the coincidence of these two entities: their derivation is purely rational. Unamuno is so adamantly anti-rational that he negates the reality of both entities. The "cogito" part is no more than a thinking reality that is aware of itself thinking, existing not in the world of physical phenomena but in the conceptual world of the mind, and the "sum" is a self derived from the cogito and therefore, that much more unreal. The notion of the self is an abstraction, and the significance of Descartes' proposition is reduced to theoretical nothingness: "I think, therefore I think I am thinking existence.

Unamuno's obsession for the existential philosophy is derived from his awareness of death, and not *vice versa.* His distrust and eventual rejection of

Cartesian rationalism leads to the most irrational and most precarious of all intellectual-emotional positions: the negation of the power of death through "faith in faith itself." Unamuno appeals to the superior being regardless of reason. His confidence in God--a confidence wrought by desperation--forms the basis of agonistic faith and creates the mainspring of his vital religion. Life is a continual struggle between yes and no. In the end, Unamuno begs: "Senor, dame la duda..los creyentes son los que matan Dios." (Lord, give me doubt..the believers are the ones who kill God.[1] Unamuno places all his bets on the absurd existence of God, on the absurd hope of immortality. Certainty and syllogism are the agents of death. They can be eluded only by preserving the mystery, heightening the paradox, creating the vitality of tortured self-doubts. Unamuno's salvation from death is his own Promethian struggle for uncertainty and his rejection of all forms of assertion. And death-- the only certainty -- is the source of all his turmoil.

References

Choron, Jacques. _Death and Western Thought._ New York: Crowell-Collier Publishing Company, 1963.

Ilie, Paul. _Unamuno: An Existential View of Self and Society._ Madison: University of Wisconsin Press, 1967.

Unamuno, Miguel de. _Del Sentimiento Tragico de la Vida._ Buenos Aires: Espana-Calpe,1950. (_The Tragic Sense of Life._ New York: Dover Publications,1954. First published in 1921).

Unamuno, Miguel de. _Obras Completas._ Madrid: Afrodisio Aguado,1959.

1 Professor Juan Marischal quoting Unamuno in Humanities Lecture 55 given at Harvard,February 18, 1969.

PART VI

FILMS AND BOOKS ON DEATH

Chapter 16

Romantic Death in "Elvira Madigan"

Jean McGarry

"Sad is this death. It goes its way in broad daylight with a sun flooding everything with a light of pure gold."

"Suicide is a way of thwarting outside forces that are making living impossible."

The grossly diverse nature, tone and objective of these two quotations --the first from Van Gogh, the other by psychoanalyst Gregory Zilboorg--epitomize a basic dichotomy regarding attitudes and perspective on death and suicide. The relevance or value of one view over another --romantic oneness with nature and the cosmos or the fatal relinquishing of being and consciousness --are issues which the viewer of the motion picture _Elvira Madigan_ must grapple with as an integral part of his esthetic reaction to the film. To adhere to a "realistic" view, the viewer must extricate himself from the subtle and seductive maneuvers of the director, which are aimed at leading him to accept the romantic philosophy of death. For example, the logic, imagery and music are closely bound up in the visual and emotional justification of the artist's fundamental attitude toward death; thereby creating conditions for a strong and absolute embracing or acceptance of the total film impact, with no allowance for a middle or halfway ground. Esthetically, and philosophically, the film takes a firm stand for the romantic side of death and suicide. In this paper, both aspects of the dilemma on death perspective will be explored. To achieve this, the film will be treated first from an objective, scientific and naturalistic standpoint, outside the realm of subtle archetypal imagery; and secondly, the montage of emotions, symbols and interactions will be described and interpreted within the framework of the artistry of music and lyrical landscape.

First of all, the case of Elvira and Sixtan will be reviewed as a psychological autopsy, revealing relevant historical, social, interactional and situational factors, operant in their demise. It appears that Sixtan first shot Elvira and then himself, in a premeditated effort. Both people were found to be suffering advanced starvation, although a basket of untouched food was found near the bodies. The couple had, a month earlier, abandoned their careers, families and towns.

She was formerly a circus performer, renowned and enamoured by all who had seen her artful tightrope dancing. She left behind deeply saddened family and admirers, to travel with a man she had met at the circus. Sixtan had defected from the Swedish military. He is survived by a wife and two children, whom he abandoned to join Elvira Madigan. From their day of departure, they were stalked by those who were to convict Sixtan and return Elvira to the circus. Several persons recognized them while they were in hiding and their evidence aided in the reconstruction of the events of this month. From these data, one can speculate about the causes of their pre-necessary death. (The following comments go beyond the scope of the coroner or psychologist who follows up the case. At this point, all the facts and exposition in the film will be assumed.)

Theories can well be generated by applying certain historical and sociological concepts to the events in the film, eventually narrowing the scope of the review to include situational, and behavioral criteria (prodromata which predict imminent suicide). First of all, Sixtan Sparr was an officer of the Royal Swedish army, an elite, honored arm of the government. A close examination of this organization and its role in the society provides a general perspective on the whole of Swedish society from which implications on its effects on the individual can be drawn. Strongly integrated and of an authoritarian style, the military boasted the flower of Sweden's manhood, in its ranks. Intelligent and carefully selected to be culturally and physically "superior" to the rank and file of the general population, the soldiers renounced their individuality and freedom to comply with the "higher good" of the military, reflected in the degree of one's loyal obedience and disciplined submission to the superiors of the military hierarchy and ultimately to the authority of the king. Strongly tradition-directed and nationalistic, they embodied an altruistic spirit and esprit de corps shared to a lesser degree by the general populace. The severe, rigidly structured military society abhored violations of the sacred duty to country and to the permanence of the bonds of wedlock. However, despite the strongly legitimized solidarity and integration in the society, a case can be made about the failure of this tight structure to bind human individuation and free choice. For example, there was a higher suicide rate for eliteist, highly establishmentarian officers of the military than any other single group (or the general population). The taking of one's own life, in a situation where one does not control his life but relegates his autonomy to his superiors, is an act of individual rebellion and disgust with the system and one's participation in it. Sixtan Sparr dares to desert this possessive organization, in an act of social suicide. He strips himself of military, familial and social roles by divesting himself of brass buttons and braid. The past is obliterated in the symbolic denial of his identity in that existence, when he relinquishes his name and his beard. A new identity and appearance facilitate orientation and passage into a new life of freedom and intimacy. Similarly, Elvira enacts the death and rebirth ritual in her adoption of the name Hedwig and the renouncing of family and the circus. Elvira and Sixtan live together, leaving in their wake, on the one hand, infamy, and on the other, romance and mystification. Alienated from society and defying its superego demands, they become a special world to themselves, evincing their own values and rules. This life is opted for, not without risk, just as their former careers were distinctly dangerous undertakings. Both learned to live with the possibility of imminent death; she experienced a near-fatal fall and he, the ravages of battle. Death, therefore, was neither a fearful spectre nor a horror.

Death and suicide are fairly germane to their situation. When Sixtan is informed of his wife's attempted suicide, he is not particularly shocked or moved to rush to her side. Threats to their integrity and their authenticity and morality of their new situation (as in this event) fail to coax them to return to society and social responsibility. Their resolution of the forces impinging upon them complies with the philosophy and mores of their dyadic cosmos. Their loyalties are solely to each other and are consonant with a world whose standard of meaning and perspective is a blade of grass.

The strength and pervasiveness of their fidelity to this code is illustrated in the pub incident. In this case, their devotion creates a tense situation in which they are faced with the choice of gaining money and food for survival and jeopardizing the innocence and purity of their love, or starving to preserve their idyllic world. This conflict is resolved by the latter decision, but the delicate interpersonal network of Elvira and Sixtan is increasingly invaded by the threat of capture by the military police. The stress between their ideals and the demand of nature and society lead to recurring conflicts. They cannot physically survive without the help of economy and production of society (especially in winter); they cannot endure life within the society, and they refuse to watch each other slowly die from starvation and cold. These are the conflicts whose eventual resolution bring about the death of Elvira and Sixtan.

Their end was an intentioned death wrought to fend off subintentioned starvation and a subintended fatal situation. Moreover their life and death together was of a higher absolute value than longevity of misery. A close examination of behavioral and situational prodromata will reveal the rate of change and intensity in their intent to commit suicide. Two distinct phases of perturbation are noteworthy: the listlessness and irritation of aggravated hunger and the sudden calm and quiet tranquility in evidence immediately before they died. However, these fluctuations must be seen within the context of a sudden radically altered life, founded after a basic and ultimately significant life decision had been made. The dangerous situation and its double-bound character created a state of lethality, increased by the dire prophecies of the fortune teller and the insistent pleas of Elvira for the acceptance of the final solution (suicide).

The soldier and the beautiful tightrope dancer were to be legendary figures: Sixtan Sparr, the epitome of the "ideal" Swedish man and father, and Elvira Madigan, as the cold princess of the ropes. The fantasy and romantic beauty of their post-selves would eventually be appreciated by a more lenient, less repressive society. For the society in which they lived, for coroners and for the soldiers, the cocoon of their blissful life together is impenetrable because of the blinders of moralism and authoritarianism. To the lovers, the tragic end is most appropriate: It brought an end to the life-virtue-love-death conflicts, as well as preserved their love relationship until the end. Sparr speaks of living in a woman's world of green grass and butterflies where contentment and peace reign supreme. In death, as in life, they remain at one with each other: the consummation of a life wish. Hence their death was prenecessary but appropriate.

Van Gogh in describing death through his painting of a golden cornfield uses verbal and visual imagery studded with allusions to endless time and immortality. A similar metaphor is employed in the symbols of the film in order to paint a picture of a romantic and natural death. It is the objective of this section of the paper to elucidate the significance of these symbols as they reflect upon the intentions of the artist-director. As a basis for this analysis Jung's theory of archetypical symbols will be employed as they unfold a sense of the natural, universal and cosmic in death.

One of the first observations that was made was the evidence for the case of a "Harlequin death" interpretation in the demise of the lovers. Women are said to approach death in a receptive, anticipatory manner, as if awaiting the arrival of a colorful and ardent lover. Hence, there is a tendency to romanticize death and to view it as the final and eternal ecstasy. In the film, the woman suggests suicide twice against the resistance of the man. Secondly, Elvira meets death in a joyful dance within a radiant sunlit environment. Sixtan, on the other hand, has the ugly task of killing her. However, this killing has overtones of "taking her"--sparing her being robbed of her innocence by the lascivious men in the pub. Sixtan has accepted this alternative suicide in view of the fact that his choices are limited to participation in a slow, debilitating starvation (a situation in which he was impotent) or death for both, by his own hand.

Death as rebirth and restitution is another notion implicit in the imagery of the film. The concept includes such things as cultural death, seasonal death and personal death, as a necessary means and requirement for new vitality and life. The independent actions of Elvira and Sixtan are a threatening influence on the tradition-directed, agrarian culture with its stronghold on disciplined submission to authority. The infamy of their act will work to loosen the rigidity, unquestioned control of individualism characteristic of the society and offer the possibility of other alternatives to life. Secondly, the change of seasons with the dying of the summer is contemporaneous with the death of the lovers. The inevitable cycle of seasons with the promise of spring renewed, symbolically assures the generation of free, alive people, ideas and love to revitalize the culture. In addition to presenting symbolic credence to the collective immortality of man through the metaphor of the seasonal cycle, a personal immortality is hinted at, through the presence of food at the death scene, as if they were preparing for a journey and a place beyond. A child's perspective on death is intimated here, as it (death) is compared to departure or sleep: cessation does not seem consonant with this scenario. After the sounds of shells are heard, there is no realistic death scene. Instead, Elvira is depicted in a permanent flight of dance with butterflies. The last frame of the film is a snapshot which permanently locks her image in the mind and heart of Sixtan. The photograph and its effects bring us to another significant aspect of the pervasiveness of the director's philosophy, expressed through esthetic means. The viewer is given the eyes of the lover through ingeniously subtle photography. Elvira is seen through Sixtan's eyes, as the camera is placed on the same level with her, a few feet away. Impressionistic fuzziness, distortion of motion and special color effects contribute to the personalized, subjective vision of the girl, as the beloved. Therefore, when she 'dies' arrested in space and time, her vision is internalized in the viewer's mind. Impressionist painting captured the fleeing and momentary and preserved it in colors and shapes on canvas; similarly, impressionistic photography renders the lover, immortalized in the last "frame" (moment) of her life. The viewer is well prepared for this final shot of her death by the cumulative effect of earlier slow-motion techniques and supercolor brilliance. He is powerfully swept away with this artistry and finds himself ultimately receptive to their playful existence of unreality, as well as emotionally and visually prepared (because of this foreshadowing of fantasy) for the imaginary, playful aspects of their death. Desertion, starvation and suicide are made palatable under the disarming guise of a Mozart piano concerto's yellow brilliance and lyrical summer landscape.

Related to this visual and auditory seduction of the mind is the generous application of more recondite groups of symbols in the imagery. An attempt was made to amalgamate certain symbols under a common heading in the hopes of finding their collective thematic significance, as they occur in the sequence of the plot. Fishing, herbs and eggs form one group, focusing on food; a critical issue. Fishing symbolizes the sacred pathway that leads from man's spiritual essence to his outer consciousness. Elvira and Sixtan are successful fishermen in both the literal and figurative senses. In the latter case, they have fused the essence of humanness, love and freedom, with their perceptions, attitudes and life style. The herbs signify a natural force for good and evil; that is, medicinal and poisonous. This describes the tenor of their lives in which they comply to life with an affinity for the natural order of things, and an acceptance of their fate. Eggs are an especially noteworthy Swedish symbol of immortality and generativity. Interestingly enough, this food is especially added as part of the sustenance they bring to their death.

A second group of symbols are related to sunlight, clearly a dominant image in the film. In this category, flowers, butterflies, radiance and golden hair are included. Yellow flowers and hair are part of the sun symbolism and are metaphors of the soul flooded with light. Radiance signifies some supernatural message, wrought against a neutral or negative background. The untimely and beautiful love of Elvira and Sixtan, in an era that renounces and attempts to stamp it out, could be the message that nudged the neutral-negative background of Sweden to liberalize and liberate its people. The butterfly is an insect attracted to light, but it also lies in fear for the winged foot that will crush out its life, as it dances a pattern of conjugal love and rebirth. Elvira is the beautiful butterfly who awaits the inevitable death from society and nature. The juxtaposition of these three metaphors with the two lovers places the human on the order of primordial life-spirits and archetypal symbols.

A final group of symbols revolves around the notions of time and death. The river symbolizes a creative source as well as oblivion and endless time. "Time is a river without banks." Elvira's dance signifies her passage into timelessness, and a union of space and time. Death itself is a metaphor for immortality and for release and transcendence of the strictures of the over-civilized order and socialization, and the structure of architectural order. Finally, unendurable tension is certainly a critical issue in the demise of Elvira and Sixtan, for which death is the liberation.

A final note on symbolism might include the role of the beautiful piano concerto, Number 21 in C Major, by Mozart. The second movement, or Andante, is the recurring musical theme of the film. It is a gentle piece which encloses within its sweet and calm warmth a golden piercing chord which complements the tranquil surrounding melody. It is like a golden-haired girl who is part of a tender, playful dream but carries a foreboding note of imminent tragedy. The piece ends dramatically with great force and brilliance, perfectly consonant with the final frames of the film. This romantic music is another artistic element used to beguile the viewer to the dreamlike acceptance of death.

Imagery, symbolism, characterization, music and plot are manipulated by the artist-director who created Elvira Madigan. These elements interact with and complement each other, resulting in a beautiful, expressive, esthetic whole with an implicit and tight philosophical structure. The first part of this paper attempted to expose the obvious and objective (factual) elements of the story line through the tools and concepts of sociology, psychology and suicidology. This analysis led to the justification of the suicide on the grounds of appropriateness, natural deterministic factors, life style of the victims and social structure of Sweden (nineteenth century). The second part of the paper dealt with the psychic, emotional level of the imagery and symbolization, giving deep, cosmic sympathy and awareness of the universal significance of the death event.

The manner in which these two perspectives align themselves around the issue of suicide and death reflects my own reactions and ruminations about the film, the first and second times I saw it. I experienced deep resistance to the suicide with its rational and lyrical justification, after the first viewing, while a second exposure totally enchanted me and rendered me completely sympathetic to the viewpoint of the director. Hence, I join with Van Gogh in the conclusion:

> "Sad is this death. It goes its way in broad daylight with a sun flooding everywhere with a light of pure gold."

Chapter 17

The Bardo Thodol or Tibetan Book of the Dead

Joseph Pulitzer IV

The Bardo Thodol, or Tibetan Book of the Dead, first translated into English in 1927, is an ancient Tibetan text conceived as a spiritual and intellectual guide for the soul or spirit of one deceased. It deals with after-death experiences, or the experiencing of reality during the various stages of the Bardo existence following death preceding rebirth. More than this, however, the text serves to illustrate the fundamental cultural dichotomy between East and West not only in content and purpose, but through the symbolism and psychology involved in the overall metaphysical assertion which provides the motivation and need for this doctrine. In this sense then, The Tibetan Book of the Dead offers a unique and important contribution to the study of death, particularly the psychology of death, for while various cultures and races have separately recognized the significance of death, only in this document can one find an accessible psychological means to a spiritual end, enlightenment, completely compatible and integrated with its contemporary cultural cosmology.

Perhaps the greatest achievement of this text, and also a necessary realization in appreciating its content, is its total communion of psychology and philosophy. As Jung makes clear in his psychological commentary on the text, "Metaphysical assertions are statements of the psyche, and are therefore psychological." The importance of this doctrine is two-fold. First, the whole definition of reality is reduced to a product of the consciousness of each individual, an assumption completely in accordance with the Maya Buddhist philosophy propounded in this text. (Jung, p.xxxvii)

> "The ever-present, unspoken assumption of the Bardo Thodol is the anti-nominal character of all metaphysical assertions, and also the idea

> of the qualitative difference of the various levels of consciousness and of the metaphysical realities conditioned by them."

In other words, the consciousness of an individual is his absolute reality, and the world he lives in, the phenomena of projections surrounding him, are merely illusions. To realize this is to obtain enlightenment. (Evans-Wentz,1927, p.104):

> "Recognize the voidness of thine own intellect to be Buddhahood, and knowing it at the same time to be thine own consciousness, thou shalt abide in the state of the Divine mind of the Buddha."

Secondly, and more importantly, this realization reflects the duality of Eastern philosophy, the total integration of selfhood with spiritual enlightenment, the communion of spiritual and physical concerns. (Jung,p.xxxvii):

> "The background of this unusual book is not the niggardly European 'either-or', but a magnificently affirmative 'both-and'.

In the end, this integration is the ultimate purpose of this text. It is read to the dying man both during and after his death to orient his consciousness to the Bardo plane, to impress upon him the recognition of his own consciousness as the maker and experiencing subject of all reality, and to hopefully liberate this consciousness from the cycle of Karmic rebirth through this realization.

The supra-temporality of the soul, a belief upon which this text is founded, is compatible with Western philosophical and religious standards, yet its logical counterpart and conclusion, the doctrine of rebirth as the ultimate fulfillment of the Law of Karma, remains an enigma to Western conception, and represents perhaps the greatest cultural barrier between Eastern and Western spiritual concern. This belief in rebirth is the fundamental cause of the Tibetan Book of the Dead, just as escape from rebirth is its ultimate objective. (Jung,p.xxxviii):

> "It is the soul, which by the divine creative power inherent in it, makes the metaphysical

assertion; it posits the distinction between metaphysical entities. Not only is it the condition of all metaphysical reality, it is that reality."

In accepting the consciousness as reality, one naturally confronts the ensuing question of spiritual progression, or rather, the levels of consciousness representing the path to enlightenment. It is here that the Law of Karma presents itself as the answer and scale at once. Dr. W. Y. Evans-Wentz, the editor of the text, in his introduction to the text, elucidates the esoteric interpretation of the rebirth doctrine found underlying the goal of this work. The Bardo, or after death plane, is conceived as an illusory plane of spiritual evolution or retrogression depending upon the previous karma of the deceased. The consciousness of the deceased is in a transitory state where liberation is possible at any moment through recognition of consciousness as the creator and experience of all reality, or rather, illusory phenomena. The Bardo experiences represent a spiritual initiation in reverse, for the consciousness is confronted with the Clear Light of Reality at the very moment of death, and from this plane descends gradually through the Bardo until, being attracted by the sexual vision of mating couples, it enters a womb and is thus reborn in the illusory world of existence. For the West, this descent seems paradoxical, but it is the sustaining doctrine of karmic rebirth which explains this seemingly reverse order of experience. The point is that a consciously controlled death, possible only through yogic concentration and one-pointedness of mind, can result in a recognition of the Clear Light of Reality and liberation. For the layman, however, less adept at concentration, this book serves as a guide for the consciousness to avoid spiritual retrogression and to seek a proper rebirth in human form in order to continue on the Path towards liberation.

Spiritual retrogression, according to Evans-Wentz, implies rebirth upon a lower level of consciousness, but in the same physical form. Physical evolution or retrogression, he maintains, is a product of time, ages, in fact. Thus, men are reborn men, in spite of symbolic representations of various levels of consciousness present in the text. This esoteric interpretation of the rebirth doctrine provides a necessary key to understanding the goal of this text, for its concern is solely with spiritual rebirth, the advance hopefully made by the consciousness towards unity and recognition of reality, providing the escape from the karmic cycle of death and rebirth. This rebirth doctrine is most aptly explained in the words of T. H. Huxley (1894,p.61), who says;

> "Everyday experience familiarizes us with the facts which are grouped under the name of heredity. Every one of us bears upon him obvious marks of his parentage, perhaps of remoter relationships. More particularly, the sum of tendencies to act in a certain way, which we call 'character'-this moral and intellectual essence of man-does veritably pass over from one fleshy tabernacle to another, and does really transmigrate from generation to generation. In the new-born infant, the character of the stock lies latent, and the Ego is little more than a bundle of potentialities. But, very early, these become actualities; from childhood to age they manifest themselves in dullness or brightness-weakness or strength-viciousness or uprightness; and with each feature modified by confluence with another character, if by nothing else, the character passes on to its incarnation in new bodies. The Indian philosophers called character, as thus defined, 'karma'...In the theory of evolution, the tendency of a germ to develop according to a certain specific type, e.g. of the kidney bean seed to grow into a plant having all the characteristics of Phaseolus vulgaris, is its 'karma'. It is the 'the last inheritor and the last result' of all the conditions that have affected a line of ancestry which goes back for many millions of years, to the time when life first appeared on earth...
> As Prof. Rhys-Davids aptly says, the snowdrop 'is a snowdrop and not an oak, and just that kind of snowdrop, because it is the outcome of the Karma of an endless series of past existences.'"

The acceptance of this higher rebirth doctrine, while not really in accordance with the dualistic thinking of most Western metaphysical doctrines, points to yet another element of Eastern psychology incorporated in the conception and objective of this text. Dr. C. G. Jung, in his psychological commentary, denotes an interpretation of the Bardo Thodol as an "initiation process whose purpose it is to restore to the soul the divinity it lost at birth." This process, he maintains, is, for the West, an initiation in reverse order. Comparing it to the Western counterpart, the undergoing of analysis, Jung asserts the reality of the subconscious, finding Freudian psychology, which can only penetrate to the Sidpa Bardo of pre-uterine existence, ultimately unsatisfactory. The hallucinatory Choynid Bardo, representing the bulk of the forty-nine day period, Jung associates with a state of unchecked subconscious awareness, which in real life would probably be classified as psychosis. Speaking of the Wrathful Visions which occur during the Choynid Bardo Jung (p.xlvii) says:

> "These tortures aptly describe the real nature of the danger: it is a disintegration of the wholeness of the Bardo body, which is a kind of 'subtle body' constituting the visible envelope of the psychic self in the after-death state. The psychological equivalent of this dismemberment is psychic dissociation. In its deleterious form it would be schizophrenia (split mind). This most common of all mental illnesses consists essentially in a marked abaissment du niveau mental which abolishes the normal checks imposed by the conscious mind and thus gives unlimited scope to the play of the unconscious 'dominants'".

Continuing his initiation in reverse, Jung comes to the conclusion that the transition from Sidpa Bardo to Choynid Bardo signifies loss of ego. "It is a sacrifice of the ego's stability and a surrender to the extreme uncertainty of what must seem like a chaotic riot of phantasmal forms." In other words of Jung, "the Choynid Bardo is the equivalent of a deliberately induced psychosis." (p.xlvi). It is here that thought falters. Sacrifice of the ego is perhaps the furthest polarity between Eastern and Western thought. The concept of selfhood, individuality, and will is, in the contemporary psychology of the West, the paramount and crucial concern in the harmonious development of an individual. (Jung, p.xlvii):

"When Freud coined the phrase that the ego was 'the true seat of anxiety,' he was giving voice to a very true and profound intuition. Fear of self-sacrifice lurks deep in every ego, and this fear is often the precariously controlled demand of the unconscious forces to burst out in full strength. No one who strives for selfhood (individuation) is spared this dangerous passage, for that which is feared also belongs to the wholeness of the self--the sub-human or supra-human world of psychic 'dominants' from which the ego originally emancipated itself with enormous effort, and then only partially, for the sake of a more or less illusory freedom."

Yet it is this very selfhood, this limited consciousness of the ego, which prevents the individual from realizing reality, entrapping him in a restricted plane of reality, the product of his own consciousness. Herein lies the major premise and spiritual objective of The Tibetan Book of the Dead, to serve as a guide to a man's consciousness freed from ego by death, to orient this consciousness in order to prevent fear of self-created illusions resulting in "an ever-deepening descent into illusion and obscuration, down to the ultimate degradation of new physical rebirth." Mystics and saints, throughout the ages, have managed, through means such as yoga, fasting, sensory deprivation, and, recently, mind-expanding drugs such as mescaline and LSD, to achieve altered states of consciousness terrifying to men of ordinary cognitive awareness. In these various states of consciousness, men are able to perceive the divine reality inherent in every phenomena of life. Death, for the Tibetans, is not only a positive means of experiencing such an altered state of consciousness, but a means of escaping this illusory world of rebirth. Death, then, is not an "end," but a "beginning," an initiation process, an introduction to higher realms of consciousness wherein one is freed from the ego's inhibited perception. Aldous Huxley (1927,p.34), in relating his mescaline experience in The Doors of Perception, supports the theory advanced by Bergson and says,

"The suggestion is that the function of the brain and nervous system and sense organs is in the main eliminative and not productive. Each person is at each moment capable of remembering all that has ever happened to him and of perceiving everything that is happening everywhere in the universe. The function of the brain and nervous system is to protect us from being overwhelmed and confused by this mass of largely useless and irrelevant knowledge, by shutting out most of what we should otherwise perceive or remember at any moment, and leaving only that very small and special selection which is likely to be practically useful."

Here Huxley is speaking of an expanded consciousness acquired by the use of the drug mescaline. He goes on to say that his brain's eliminative functions were impaired, thus enabling him to perceive more; his senses being highly receptive, he was able to perceive the "Suchness" of all things. Through his experiences Huxley gained a broader definition of reality, the ultimate reality being the Voidness symbolized by the Clear Light at the Moment of death.

Expanded consciousness can perhaps be interpreted as a higher plane of awareness, a step upwards on the Path towards liberation, but this is merely the state of Karmic illusion through which the consciousness journeys during the Bardo existence after death. The whole goal of the Tibetans is to escape this illusion by recognizing it as the product of one's consciousness, which one is in good position to do, unhampered by the eliminative functions of the ego.

The ordinary consciousness of man, however, remains unable to obtain this recognition without previous training in concentration through meditation and other yogic practices involving the self-discipline of spiritual refinement. The Clear Light, which most cannot bear to recognize and flee from, is followed by a Secondary Clear Light, the ultimate reality being conceived in terms of each individual's previous consciousness. If left unrecognized, which is the probable case, the fading vision of this conceptualized truth heralds the end of the first and highest plane of the Bardo, called the Chikhai Bardo, where one is set face to face with reality. From this level, the consciousness descends to the Choynid Bardo, the hallucinatory realm of his subconscious 'dominants.'

Here liberation is also possible, through recognition of the various symbolic hallucinations signifying various "thought-forms;" the peaceful dieties being those from the psychic center of heart representing emotional impulses, and the wrathful dieties symbolizing rational, conceptualizing psychic center of the brain standing for intellectual impulses, further from reality and a realization of reality than pure feelings, which are not completely a conscious conceptualization.

The dream-state of the Choynid Bardo asserts the Buddhist doctrine of self, that each and every consciousness is Reality, Truth and Enlightenment, at the same time isolated yet at one with all. This is yet another paradox for Western thinking, but it is the natural conclusion of Buddhist psychology which, by virtue of its dualism, is able to harmoniously integrate the various metaphysical poles such as self or consciousness and reality, life as a spiritual exercise, man and "God" and birth and death, concepts which Western thought, founded upon a practical physical materialism, has isolated into absolute and incompatible dichotomies. In fact, the ultimate objective of The Tibetan Book of The Dead, and of all Eastern philosophy, is largely an antithesis of Western intellectual and philosophical values, for complete sacrifice of all intellectual and rational functioning seems a goal whose formulation, realization, and motivation are completely dependent upon that which it seeks to eliminate, conceptual activity of the mind. Yet this seemingly paradoxical and self-destructive goal is the natural conclusion of the metaphysical premises of Karma and the dualistic doctrine of spiritual isolation in unity. (Huxley,1927,p.95):

> "Thine own intellect, which is now voidness, yet not to be regarded as of the voidness of nothingness, but as being the intellect itself, unobstructed, shining, thrilling, and blissful, is the very consciousness, the All-good Buddha."

The "Void" described here implies creative awareness, absolute perception with a complete absence of cognitive conceptualization. As Jung (p.xxxix) describes this state,

> "This realization is the Dharma-Kaya state of perfect enlightenment; or, as we should

> express it in our own language, the creative ground of all metaphysical assertion is consciousness, as the invisible, intangible manifestation of the soul. The "Voidness" is the state transcendent over all assertion and predication."

The "Voidness," then, is not a blank and formless cessation of consciousness, but absolute creation and awareness, an experience inconceivable to ordinary minds. Again, it is a dualistic concept, the absence of formative activity equated with absolute creation and awareness, and inexplicable in logical terms.

Yet this state of enlightenement, the Dharma-Kaya, is a distant goal, and, though the ultimate objective of this text, other preparations for the karmic descent to physical rebirth are carefully laid out in the third and final portion of the book, the Sidpa Bardo.

The Sidpa Bardo, which occurs during the last part of the after death experience, is when the deceased, unable to obtain liberation through recognition of The Clear Light of Reality or of his own hallucinatory thought-forms, the reality created by his Karmic propensities, must choose and enter a womb for rebirth. The process of selection is an important one, but it must be remembered that the final choice will be dictated by previous Karma, and the decision-making process is merely the first trace of illusion which is human reality.

The instructions for entering and closing the womb-door are explicit, for the very reason that rebirth in human form is essential to make conscious progress on the Path towards liberation. An esoteric interpretation, however, implies the process of avoiding spiritual retrogression, to not be born on a lower level of consciousness symbolized by the many physical and animal birth forms cautioned against in the text. In the words of Jung (p.li) again:

> "Human life, therefore, is the vehicle of the highest perfection it is possible to obtain; it alone generates the karma that makes it possible for the dead man to abide in the perpetual light of the Voidness without clinging to any object, and thus to

rest upon the hub of the wheel of rebirth, freed from all illusion of genesis and decay."

Yet liberation is eminently possible even in this, the last and final stage of the after-death Bardo world. By recognizing one's fear, culminating in the desire for a body, and abiding in a resigned state of quiescence, one is still able to obtain liberation in the Nirvana-Kaya, the level of enlightened rebirth, as a Buddha or saint. The Tri-Kaya doctrine, one of the fundamental wisdoms of Buddhism, consists of the Dharma-Kaya, or state of perfect enlightenment, the Sambhoga-Kaya, or the one body that represents a physical manifestation of the ultimate reality of the Dharma-Kaya, and the Nirvana-Kaya, being the level of enlightened rebirth, for the aid of men trapped in the world of illusion, isolated from Nirvana, or the Dharma-Kaya. The symbolic trilogy, as in the cosmology of Christianity, has both an esoteric interpretation and an esoteric significance as well. The various levels of the trinity, according to Dr. Evans-Wentz, are merely to denote the difference and separation between "God", "clergy", and "layman," or rather, between the Universal Creation and Reality, the Indescribable Dharma-Kaya, its embodiment and manifestation, the Sambhoga-Kaya, and its exponent in human from, the teacher or Buddha, of the Nirvana-Kaya. Yet this division entails no qualitative difference among the forms of enlightenment, for such distinctions of any sort are transcended naturally in the realization of liberation. In the words of Lama Kazi Dawa-Samdup, reknowned guru and translator of this text (Evans-Wentz,1927,p.13):

> "In the boundless panorama of the existing and visible universe, whatever shapes appear, whatever sounds vibrate, whatever radiances illuminate, or whatever consciousnesses cognize, all are the play or manifestation of the Tri-Kaya, the Three-fold Principle of the Cause of All Causes, the Primordal Trinity. Impenetrating all is the All-Pervading Essence of Spirit, which is Mind. It is uncreated, impersonal, self-existing, immaterial, and indestructible."

The significance of the Wisdom Teachings, such as the Tri-Kaya Doctrine lies not so much in their symbolism, or esoteric interpretation, but in their contribution to the psychology underlying the whole structure of this text. While the religious Tibetan has probably acquired a personal meaning of these myths and doctrines over a lifetime of spiritual concern, the fact remains that esoterically, they exist. In other words, a highly detailed, comprehensive symbolic superstructure has been created with a precise cosmology, geography, and nomenclature, similar, in fact, to almost every Eastern religion, with each sect having evolved its unique illustration and explanation of the universe and its history. Obviously, it is a product of many centuries of conscious refinement, with each episode and name symbolic of a spiritual function. Tentatively, this intricate web of stories, names, episodes, and achievements could be defined as the end product of sociological, rather than intellectual, evolution. Under such a structural analysis, emphasis centers upon the reverse of the logical process, concentrating upon the end as shaping the means. In this case, the mythical structure seems to have its origin among the people, and not the lamas, for while the Tibetan Book of The Dead was kept by lamaist tradition in secrecy by "the Seven Seals of Silence" for centuries, its origin dates back to Bon influences, the pre-Buddhist religion in Tibet. Such antiquity can mean only one thing. This mythical structure, religious in origin, evolved as an explanation for the universe and its functions that would identify the illusory values and "realities" of earth existence with planes higher, thus giving the people, who, uneducated or uncaring, could not comprehend consciously the metaphysical aims of Buddhism, a whole life-line with which they could identify and in which they could immerse themselves and place their trust, thus eventually making spiritual progress. This form of religion, worship of dieties, is still practiced widely among the people of India and Tibet today, while the lamas search for spiritual truth through the higher means.

The subtle psychology of the Choynid Bardo, then, can never really be fully understandable to us, for in its symbolic functions, as Evans-Wentz asserts, this text reflects the thought and influence of both Buddhist and pre-Buddhist doctrines, and its analysis would require a lifetime of study, familiarization, and esoteric insight. Yet, in sensing its purpose, which transcends the worldly staples of existence, one is aware of the psychology involved, the psychology of almost any religion, and one can only admire the total communion of physical and spiritual concerns achieved. In many ways, this text is for the living as well as the dead. Aside from its spiritual significance in asserting the "Art of Dying," this text fulfills an emotional need for any bereaved, somewhat similar, but far more comforting, than the funeral of the West. As Jung (p.l) says:

> "This cult of the dead is rationally based on the belief in the supra-temporality of the soul, but its irrational basis is to be found in the psychological need of the living to do something for the departed. This is an elementary need which forces itself upon even the most 'enlightened' individuals when faced by the death of relatives or friends. That is why, enlightenment or no enlightenment, we still have all manner of ceremonies for the dead."

In practice, however, this means of fulfilling the need would seem far more effective, for comfort is assured by the same religious belief of rebirth and spiritual evolution as a possibility, with death as the ultimate means.

Yet the psychological functions of this book are only secondary, as Jung makes clear. The rationality of this book finds its foundations in religious faith, to many an irrational process. Yet even the most practical of materialists can not help be swayed by this document, for even with no personal spiritual concerns, one cannot help but admire the significance of death as it is symbolically portrayed in the Tibetan Book of The Dead. Whether Eastern doctrines can be termed more fulfilling or nearer the truth is debatable, for an individual must always find personal meaning and faith in whatever metaphysical doctrines he chooses to create or accept. Yet the significance of this text is universal, for death touches in some way everyone, and the philosophy and psychology underlying the Bardo Thodol represent a contribution and new direction not only to the science of death, but to every concerned person throughout the world. Its significance, just as its content and ultimate objective, is relevant to each individual in whatever revelations it determines. As Jung (p.xlvii) points out:

> "There are, and always have been, those who cannot help but see that the world and its experiences are in the nature of a symbol, and that it really reflects something that lies hidden in the subject himself, in his own transubjective reality."

This statement provides a befitting conclusion to this review: The Tibetan Book of the Dead deals with a completely subjective experience on every level. Any analysis such as this can serve only a superficial function, for its content is merely the exposition of one individual. The text is and must always remain an individual's key, whose content is to be read, meditated upon, and hopefully experienced and resolved personally within the reality of each individual. As such, from the Western standpoint, it is a relatively useless book, for it offers no tangible benefits. It provides only a key, a key to the undiscovered self that determines what is and what will be. Herein lies its value, a value of universality.

Chapter 18

Dead Ernest

Stretch Longstreth

The theme of death slices through all the major works of Ernest Hemingway. All four major novels are exercises in confrontation politics with death. Hemingway describes the physical characteristics of his opponent in revealing detail. The description creates the confrontation. Throughout his works he develops the life-death opposition approaching the end from various angles, occasionally tackling it head on.

The conflict never resolves. Hemingway cannot meet death, nor can he fight it, accept it, desire it, overcome it, or ignore it. A living being gets no relief in the confrontation with death, except through dying, a circular and thus unsatisfactory resolution. Hemingway's works do not aim at resolution, though they may pretend to for the sake of the reader. He wishes to portray life in view with its inability to compromise with death. His art reaches a very high level of frustration. The frustration is integral to his work, and he emphasizes and develops most fully that feeling in his novel *The Sun Also Rises*.

The book uses circularity as the evidence of frustration. Circular motion, circular time, circular life, all show the frustration of living. The positive title held against the background of a negative story and in context of the full quotation from *Ecclesiastes* aptly shows the eternally circular existence of total frustration.

> "One generation passeth away, and another generation cometh; but the earth abideth forever..The sun also ariseth, and the sun goeth down, and hasteth to the place where he arose."

"Turn. Turn. Turn."- The Byrds.

In the beginning the reader meets the speaker, Jake, his circle of friends and companions, and his lover, Brett. By the end the life of the major characters has not changed; their relationships return pretty much to their initial positions. Robert Cohn goes back to his wife whom he dislikes. Mike loves Brett with a bleeding heart. Brett and Jake love each other despite the fact that they can never realize union.

At one point during the novel the circle shows a chance of breaking, Brett falls in love with a young bullfighter. Yet, this episode ends just as the others, Brett calls Jake to bail her out of a mess that resolves itself before his arrival.

They drink a lot of booze to forget their existence, and find some sort of relief short of death. Booze of course is only a temporary solution that keeps them alive and in pain instead of permitting them the excess of death.

The axis of the living circle is Jake and more particularly Jake's war wound that cost him his sex (p.31):

> "That was where the liaison colonel came to visit me...Then he made that wonderful speech: 'You, a foreigner, an Englishman' (any foreigner was an Englishman) 'have given more than your life.' What a speech! I would like to have it illuminated to hang in the office. He never laughed. He was putting himself in my place, I guess. 'Che mala fortuna! Che mala fortuna!'"

War, death's agent, has robbed Jake of his ability to make love. Love, then, never exists for him as a possibility of opposition to death.

In contrast to the loveless existence of the Lost Generation are the bullfighters and their surrounding culture. The bullfighter lives, uses up every drop of his life. He confronts death every time he enters the ring. The bull always dies even if the matador cannot kill him, and the rest of the bullfight builds on this basis or fact. The ritualistic play develops around the death of the bull with the matador as the chief character. He kills at the risk of his own body and his own life, but not as in a game. The bull never receives an equal chance nor is his life ever spared. The outcome of the fight is predetermined even before the start; the sport lies in the execution of fate.

Hemingway devoted an entire book to his favorite art, Death in the Afternoon. The book mostly describes bullfighting and all of its parasitic cultures. In it also though Hemingway explains his fascination for the sport and gives his view of death in the process(p.2).

> "The only place where you could see life and death, *i.e*. violent death now that the wars were over, was in the bull ring and I wanted very much to go to Spain where I could study it. I was trying to learn to write, commencing with the simplest things, and one of the simplest things of all and the most fundamental is violent death. It has none of the complications of death by disease or so-called natural death, or the death of a friend or some one you have loved or have hated, but it is death nevertheless, one of the subjects that a man may write of."

In the bull fight, life and death meet and conflict just as man on foot and wild beast meet and conflict. These are the central actions of the tragedy. The matadors intend to live, not to die, and their death is accidental. The death of the horses is incidental, for they perform as the comic relief (p.7):

> "The comic that happens to these horses is not their death then; death is not comic, and gives a temporary dignity to the most comic characters, although this dignity passes once death has occurred; but the strange and burlesque visceral accident which occur."

Matadors frequently get wounded, and the best seem to die in the ring even though the plot does not inherently include this action. But death under the sun naturally suits the bullfighter who lives fully by repeatedly introducing himself to his alternative. He has chosen to use his life up in one ecstatic blast instead of painfully drawing it out over years of age.

At one point in the book Hemingway adds a short piece of insight into his death view. He entitles it "A Natural History of the Dead." Most of it ridicules the Christian notion of afterlife based on faith as expressed by Mungo Park while starving in Africa in regards to a small plant which he had found in an otherwise most barren desert (p.134):

> "Can that Being who planted, watered and brought to perfection, in this obscure part of the world, a thing which appears of so small importance, look with unconcern upon the situation and suffering of creatures formed after his own image? Surely not."

To this Hemingway opposes the Naturalist's view, disinterested description (p.137):

> "Until the dead are buried they change somewhat in appearance each day. The color change in Caucasian races is from white to yellow, to yellow-green, to black. If left long enough in the heat the flesh comes to resemble coal-tar, especially where it has been broken or torn, and it has quite a visible tar-like iridescence."

Ernest depicts his friend, Death, in very physical terms, as the oh so grinning butcher. Death is just that, the end, nothing more. The philosophy of his works turns on the various ways to deal with that inevitable fact.

The popularity of A Farewell to Arms rests mostly on its beauty as a communication of love. Hemingway sets up love in opposition to war, the agent of violent death. Love seems to be a very real answer. Fred and Catherine lose themselves in their love for each other and forget the rest of the violent world.

Halfway through the novel Hemingway lays death on the idyllic scene in the form of rain. The use of rain as a death symbol links the womb and death desires. This union forbodes Catherine's end while giving birth to a dead child, and the virtual death of Fred since his love and its seal no longer exist. Death proves all-powerful in destroying the love that opposed it. Fred is left like Jake with no alternatives (p.338):

> "Maybe he was choked all the time. Poor little kid. I wished the hell I'd been choked like that. No I didn't. Still there would not be all this dying to go through. Now Catherine would die. That was what you did. You died. You did not know what it was about. You never had time to learn. They threw you in and told you the rules and the first time they caught you off base they killed you. Or they killed you gratuitously like Aymo. Or gave you syphilis like Rinaldi. But they killed you in the end. You could count on that. Stay around and they would kill you."

For Whom the Bell Tolls also involves a love broken by violent death. The switch from woman to man dying or from the secondary to the primary character forces a switch from Hemingway's usual first-person to third-person speaker. The death of a man must involve a different commitment than that of woman to giving birth. The man dies for a cause, the Republic. That the cause is lost and of little merit especially to a foreigner shows its lack of importance in itself. The importance of the cause lies mainly in the man's life commitment to it. The commitment gives purpose to life, but it also overshadows and destroys love.

Robert Jordan builds a union with Maria, but he must die and his death diminishes her. She dies with him because of the completeness of their love.

When they make love they reach a cosmic oneness that they both feel as death (p.159):

> "For him it was a dark passage which led to nowhere, then to nowhere, then again to nowhere, always and forever to nowhere, heavy on the elbows in the earth to nowhere, dark never any end to nowhere, hung on all time always unknowing nowhere, this time and again for always to nowhere, now not to be home once again always and to nowhere, now beyond all bearing up, up, up and into nowhere. Suddenly, scaldingly, holdingly

all, nowhere gone and time absolutely still and they were both there, time having stopped and he felt the earth move out and away from under them."

In the union of love all becomes the present, the now-here,and the no-where. They are each other as now is then and all is nothing. They leave the earth in their union with the all and with the nought.

This idea of mutual self-destruction in the act of love gets repeated although more crudely in The Snows of Kilimanjaro. Harry, who is dying of gangrene, at one point remarks to his wife "I'd like to destroy you a few times in bed.'" (p.14). Harry later dies but remains the speaker in the story. Hemingway gives a glimpse of death; death appears as relief from the grotesque pain of life. The dead man flies off in his mind to Kilimanjaro, the great, snow-covered mountain. Water returns as a death-symbol, this time in the form of snow. Death for this man does not promise the warmth of the womb, but cold flight.

The Old Man and the Sea regards the last efforts of an old fisherman to prove that he still has life's juices pulsating through his veins. The old man has faced death throughout his life on the sea. He fishes from killing the produce of the sea, but to do so he must work on the sea and within reach of the death of the sea.

The confrontation of the old man and the sea resembles that of the matador and the bull. The old man has lived and yet has managed to weather the risks of his occupation. Now he nears natural death and his dreams prove his closeness to the end. He no longer dreams of conflict or of love, but of the peace of his youth (p.24).

> "He was asleep in a short time and he dreamed of Africa when he was a boy and the long golden beaches and the white beaches, so white they hurt your eyes, and the high capes and the great brown mountains. He lived along the coast now every night and in his dreams he heard the surf roar and saw the native boat come riding through it....He dreamed only of places now and of the lions on the beach. They played like young cats

> in the dusk and he loved them as he loved the boy."

The simple imagery shows the old man's desire for relief from the conflict of the sea through the peace of the sea. The majesty of gold and lions mixed with cold white and water resembles the picture of death drawn in <u>The Snows of Kilimanjaro</u>. Even while fighting the great fish on the sea he dreams during the few minutes of rest that he gets (p.81).

> "He did not dream of the lions but instead of a vast school of porpoises that stretched for eight or ten miles and it was in the time of their mating and they would leap high into the air and return into the same hole they had made in the water when they leaped.
>
> Then he dreamed that he was in the village on his bed and there was a norther and he was very cold and his right arm was asleep because his head had rested on it instead of the pillow."

The porpoises return to their points of entry in a circular, sexual motion just as the old man returns to his youth in dream. The future reference of sleep during a cold norther comes in at the end of the book when the old man is beaten and tired.

The sea wins at last as it must, as death must. One can fight and love and live every drop of flowing blood, but the end comes to all. <u>The Old Man and the Sea</u>, was Hemingway's last and greatest catch. It won him the Nobel Prize. But afterwards he knew that his juices were slowing that the vitality of his body would not last eternally. The legend of Ernest Hemingway would remain, though, especially with a last valiant, violent touch. Michener (Iberia, 1968, p. 498) tells us:

> "On the day the news came over the wire I went out to see Juan Belmonte (the greatest Spanish matador and compatriot of Hemingway) and told him, 'Don Ernesto just committed suicide,' and Belmonte said very slowly and very clearly, 'Well done.'"

Chapter 19

Coping with Death in Agee's _A Death in the Family_

Richard Genz

Agee's _A Death in the Family_ is a complete sociological exegesis of the effect of one death on a family and a community. In one way or another, death pervades every part of the story. Seemingly minor nuances in language in the beginning prepare the reader for the all-important death which is to come later. When Jay is awakened by the ringing telephone on which Ralph will give him news of his father's illness--news which summons Jay to his death--Jay picks up the phone in the middle of its ring and listens "with savage satisfaction to its death rattle." Throughout the book, Agee brilliantly illustrates how our anxieties about death permeate our slang ("dead right", "dead certain","dead silence", "deadly serious") in much the same way that sex does.

In addition to being a subtle indicator of our fears about death, language in the novel is an extremely important protective device for the characters who are trying to cope with them. Ralph, a very weak character, sees his father near death and thinks of him in these words: "...he lay there now, old and broken, cast aside near the end of the trail, yes sir, the embers fading....He was coming near his last hour." He formulates his thoughts in terms of cliches he has heard and used many times before in less disturbing circumstances. The "yes sir" in his thoughts clearly indicates that he is trying to protect himself from the pain of his father's illness by trying to think of it in a casual way. The fact that he has heard these cliches so many times also serves to reassure him that death is an ancient aspect of existence, that he is not going through anything new--people have experienced deaths of loved ones many times before, and they have survived the trauma.

When Jay's death becomes the central subject of the book, the same use of protective language is apparent. The country man who first calls Mary and tells her that something has gone wrong has an interesting progression in his speech; he says "There's been a slight--your husband has been in an accident... A serious accident." Though he knows her husband is dead, he starts to say it is a "slight" mishap of some kind. The strongest term he is able to use is "serious accident". Mary suspects the truth, and she extends the progression one step more by telling Andrew that Jay has been in "a very serious accident."

Even though she does suspect the worst, at first she is absolutely unable even to think the word "death", much less speak it. When she had asked whether a doctor were present, the man had only responded, "That's all right, ma'am." Mary thinks, "That can mean anything. It can mean there's a doctor there and although it's serious he has it in hand, it isn't so dreadfully bad, although he did say it's serious or it can..."--here she stops abruptly, and begins to arrange Jay's blankets. She won't allow her thoughts to reach the concept of death. She goes on and on in this way in her conversation with Aunt Hannah. Then, unexpectedly, her manner changes completely:

"'Why didn't he tell me!' Mary burst out.

'What is it?' (Aunt Hannah)

'Why didn't I ask?' She looked at her aunt in furious bewilderment. 'I didn't even ask! How serious! Where is he hurt! Is he living or dead.'"

"There it is, Aunt Hannah said to herself." (p.121) She is rebelling against the euphemisms, the words like "serious" and "accident" that were meant to protect her from pain but are not succeeding. There is still ambivalence in her attitude toward the horrible words "dead" and "death"--she has asked the question, "Is he living or dead?" in the plainest, most straightforward way, but she is unable to continue in such frank terms. "And surely if he meant the--the very worst, he'd have just said so straight out..." She wavers back and forth from euphemisms to blunt, painful honesty of thought as her conversation with Hannah continues sadly.

Agee brings out the fact that the taboo of the word death is inculcated in people from childhood.

Aunt Hannah and Mary explain the idea of death to Cathy and Rufus in the most indirect terms. "When you get old, you can be sick and not get well again...God lets you go to sleep and you can't see people any more...You wake up right away, in heaven." Concerning Jay, they simply tell them, "God put him to sleep." The children associate this euphemism with the fate of their pet rabbits and cats, which were run over and drowned. Naturally, this is hard for them to accept. "He could not imagine his father like that." "If it was in the auto, Catherine thought, then he wouldn't be in the slop jar." (p.244) When Aunt Hannah tells them Jay had an accident, Catherine thinks she is talking about an inopportune bowel movement--the confusion of one vague, polite euphemism with another. Already, Rufus and Catherine are being exposed to protective, but completely inaccurate language which no doubt Aunt Hannah and Mary also heard in their childhoods.

Like language, religion serves a protective, reassuring function for Mary, Hannah, and the many others who are affected by Jay's death. Over and over again Mary turns to her strong Catholic faith for comfort in the hour of her affliction. For her, death and her religion are inextricably connected--she crosses herself repeatedly when pondering the possibility of Joel's death very early in the novel. I've already noted how she explains death to her children in a fundamentalist-Christian way. On hearing of Jay's car-wreck, she falls to her knees and prays. She makes no secret of her reliance on God, and cries out frequently, "<u>God help me, help me</u>."

Even before the tragedy of Jay's death, we are made aware of her devout belief that there exists a God who shares her veneration for life <u>and</u> her aversion to death. Early in the novel she finds herself wishing for the death of Jay's cranky old father, whom he has gone to visit. She is shocked at the evil of her thought, and immediately goes into a long series of prayers. "Forgive my unspeakable sinful thought. Cleanse my soul for such abominations...if it be Thy will, preserve him yet awhile." This kind of reaction to one's wish for the death of another is very common, yet quite peculiar. Mary feels there is something inherently sinful about the very thought of wishing for another's death, and she is instantly impelled to seek God's forgiveness for her thought. Yet it is to the will of this same God that she attributes the ultimate cause of every death. Thus there is a great problem in her use of religion as a comforting device in the face of Jay's death: she must find a way to justify "God's will" in order to derive any comfort from her faith. After hearing of her husband's death, she cries out to God in anguish: "'Just--have a little mercy,' she sobbed. 'A little mercy.'" She says He is trying to torment her. She then screams hysterically to God for forgiveness over and over again. (pp.158-9) This conflict limits the comforting power of her faith.

Aunt Hannah, a devout Catholic like Mary, views the practice of prayer and religion in the time of crisis far more perceptively than Mary herself ever does. Seeing Mary praying, "For the first time in her life she suspected how mistakenly prayer can be used...something mistaken, unbearably piteous, infinitely malign was at large within that faithfulness." With these thoughts, Aunt Hannah stakes out the middle ground between the cynical agnosticism of Andrew and Joel and the unquestioning faith of Mary. Hannah, always a very understanding character, senses that Mary's (and her own) reliance on prayer for security might be self-deceptive, "mistaken", and "malign", but she sees also that it is psychologically useful for the maintenance of mental equilibrium. She once says that prayer "sees us through sane." (p.130)

As in the treatment of language taboos, so in regard to religion Agee places importance on the children's attitude toward what they hear from their relatives. Will the dependence on religion in times of crisis continue in their lives? A yes or no answer is impossible, but the author does indicate that Rufus and Catherine might well be more skeptical than their mother or their Great-Aunt Hannah. They are highly mistrustful of the intimidating self-assertiveness of Father Jackson. Toward the end of the story, they hear him speaking to their mother about the funeral arrangements. (He says that a Catholic funeral is impossible for Jay, since he was not a believer.) Their reactions to his voice are very revealing, and, I think, indicative of what Agee feels to be the essence of their childhood reaction to religion--a reaction which will of course shape their adult beliefs. "He spoke as if all that he said were...final, finished, perfected beyond disquisition long before he was born; and truth and eternity dwelt like clearest water in the rhythms of his language..." (p.280) "...his voice...at once enchanted and obscurely disturbed them..." We are told that the children sense that "the something to which their mother and their great aunt were devoted" is more important to them than anything else. They also realize that "the object of this devotion was not this man whom they mistrusted, but they felt that he was altogether too deeply involved in it." The crucial point is this: the children are said to understand that the introduction of this "something"--religion-- has made everything better for her, but that "everything was far worse in one way. For before, she had at least been questioning, however gently. But now she was wholly defeated and entranced, and the transition to prayer was the moment and mark of her surrender." (p.281) The children intuitively sense that it is weakness, and not sincerity of belief, that has driven her to religion. Belief in the faith has not been successfully inculcated in them, and Agee implies that they will follow in the way of their father and his relatives; i.e., they will go through personal crises like a death in the family without relying on religion to protect them. Self-protective devotion to faith will go the way of comforting language for them. Both are disturbing and confusing; Rufus and Catherine don't trust either.

Aside from religion and language, there is a third protective device which is relatively obvious, so I won't spend much time on it. It is alcohol. Mary, Hannah, and the rest use it liberally. At one point, Hannah says that for Mary to get drunk would be "the most sensible thing she could do." Again, there is no hesitation about admitting the need for protection.

Thus far we have spoken primarily of the reactions of Mary, Rufus, and Catherine--those most directly affected by Jay's death. But one of the beautiful characteristics of <u>A Death in the Family</u> is the way it reveals the behavior of the <u>entire community</u> toward a death. Though the center of attention is usually Mary and her children, we are presented with many cogent aspects of death-attitudes in other characters as well.

One such attitude is peculiar to some males in the book. For them, a death in the family is regarded chiefly as a <u>test</u>. It is an endurance trial, a chance to show just how tough you can be in the face of adversity. Andrew and Joel feel this most strongly. They try to reconcile themselves forthrightly to the inevitability of death-crises, without seeking out the aid of devices to reduce the pain. For them, death is simply and undeniably a part of "what life is." To be strong is their goal, and they face the trauma of Jay's death with all the strength they have. This passage describing Joel's thoughts expresses the idea completely. "It had been as if he had known that this or something like this was bound to happen sooner or later; and he was hardly more moved than surprised... the air felt like iron...he could taste in his mouth the sour and cold, taciturn taste of iron. Well what else are we to expect, he said to himself. What life is. He braced against it quietly to accept, endure it, relishing not only his exertion but the sullen, obdurate cruelty of the iron, for it was the cruelty which proved and measured his courage." (p.136) It is important to note that for him, all of the significance of Jay's death lies in his own reaction to it--not in any feeling of sorrow for Jay himself. In other words, death is as important for the survivors as for the deceased. He sees the death in the family primarily as a factor in the lives of those remaining, and for him there is no point in worrying about Jay as Hannah and Mary do. Joel tries to explain this to Mary: "It's a kind of test, Mary, and it's the only kind that amounts to anything. When something rotten like this happens. Then you have your choice. You start to really be alive, or you start to die. That's all." (p.149) He then realizes that she is thinking of her religion. He implores her to "take the greatest kind of care you don't just--crawl into it like a hole and hide in it."

Ralph aspires to the attitude that Joel and Andrew hold so proudly, but he is unsuccessful. He is perhaps the most pitable character in the novel. We see him as he struggles to cope with what he considers to be his father's fatal illness--the one which called his brother Jay to his death. Ralph is "in a panic of aroused responsibility." Having been brought up by Joel, he has very clear ideas of how a man should act in such dire circumstances. He should give comfort to the women; he should be confident of his ability to withstand the emotional onslaught; simply stated, he should be strong. Ralph is miserable, for he falls far short of all these qualities manifested in his father. He feels hopelessly inadequate. He relies on alcohol, sneaking shots furtively to avoid the embarrassment of revealing his weakness to the women. He has serious feelings of sexual inadequacy which rise in intensity in the reaction to his father's illness. He imagines that his wife hates to sleep with him because he is fat. "She would prefer to sleep with...<u>any</u> man, so long as his belly don't get in the way." He says over and over that he must try to be "more of a man" in the crisis. He hugs his mother several times, more for his comfort than for hers. "...he began to feel that everyone else was watching him, and knew he was no use and that his mother did not love him." (p.69) His drinking habit has strong Freudian undertones: "...he uncorked the bottle, wrapped his mouth over its mouth as ravenously as a famished baby takes the nipple..."

Thus, Agee demonstrates how a death-crisis can have the effect of bringing to a peak all the psychological frustrations within a human being, and for Ralph it leads to this pathetic realization: "Here tonight it comes like a test, a trial, one of the times in a man's life when he is needed, and can be some good, just by being a man. But I'm not a man. I'm a baby. Ralph is the baby. Ralph is the baby." (p. 72)

Father Jackson is a character of strength in something of the same manner as Andrew and Joel--the great difference being, of course, that he is religious and they are not. He is utterly confident of his rightness and his strength. He enters the Follet house as though he lives there, and consciously takes over the role of the dead father. He reprimands the children; he comforts the widow; he sits in Jay's chair "as if he thought he belonged there."

Toward the end of the novel, the reader begins to wonder whether Mary might be acquiring some of the male strength possessed by Joel and Andrew. She begins to gain control over herself, and her feelings about the whole affair begin to resemble those which Joel explained before: she finds pleasure and satisfaction in the fact that she has lived through it all. "She thought; this is simply what living is; I never realized before what it is. She thought: now I am more nearly a grown member of the human race...She thought that she had never before had a chance to realize the strength that human beings have, to endure...She thought that she had grown up almost overnight." These thoughts do ring a little falsely to the reader, who has seen Mary search out every device available to lessen the pain of her loss, and indeed she _is_ being overconfident. Moments later, she completely loses her newly-gained composure in a classic example of an "ending." She goes to leave the bedroom where she had been talking to Father Jackson: "It was when she came to the door, to walk through it, to leave this room and to leave this shape of existence forever, that realization poured upon her and overwhelmed her...with such force, such monstrous piercing weight..that she groaned...and doubled deeply over, hands to her belly, and her knee joints melted." (p.287) She can't take it alone; she lies groaning and helpless on the floor for a few minutes. Then she makes the sign of the Cross, takes Father Jackson's arm, and "Although she tried not to, she leaned on him very heavily." (p.288) Mary is still unable to live through this ordeal without the aid and comfort of her religion.

One last aspect of the novel deserves special mention: it is Agee's treatment of the idea of an "appropriate death". Andrew tells Mary that Jay died utterly unafraid. He was killed instantly; he was aware of the danger to him, and then it ended. As he puts it, "Danger...made him every inch of the man he was. And the next instant it was all over." (p.165) His expression at the time of death was "startled, resolute, and mad as hell. Not one trace of fear or pain." Mary is comforted to hear this, that her husband died without suffering or weakness. "Very appropriate," her mother says. (p.167) This conception of his death prompts her to choose the words "In his strength" for Jay's epitaph.